Who I Am in Christ
Daily Devotional

Who I Am in Christ Daily Devotional

© Copyright 2017 Rose Publishing, LLC
P. O. Box 3473
Peabody, Massachusetts 01961-3473 USA
www.hendricksonrose.com

Book Cover and Layout design by Sergio Urquiza

ISBN: 9781628623819

Printed through Asia Pacific Offset Ltd
Printed in China
November 2017, 1st Printing

This book is given to

_____

on this day

_____

Contents

Transformation: *Becoming* Who We Are

Introduction

In a 2012 interview with *ABC News*, country-music superstar Dolly Parton admitted that she once secretly entered a celebrity look-a-like contest and lost to several other Dolly impersonators! "I got the least applause," she confessed sheepishly.

While Dolly's anecdote is amusing on one level, it's disturbing on another. Almost every day, we too get confusing messages from culture about who we are. We each wrestle—all people some of the time, and some people all the time—with the question of identity. Surely, it's this question that's behind the bizarre trend to "self-identify." It also explains the recent surge in DNA testing. More than ever, people are hungry to discover facts about their ancestry and know their precise ethnicity.

When wondering, who am I? many people look *outward.* They read best-selling, self-help books. They go on pilgrimages to *find themselves.* They spend thousands of dollars at conferences with life coaches like Tony Robbins, hoping to create *a brand-new identity and life.*

In this book, we want to look *upward.* We're convinced that a healthy identity is not something we build, it's something God bestows on us, by his grace and through our faith in Jesus.

We invite you to see for yourself what God says about you in the pages of the Bible. We think you'll agree that an identity *in Christ* is not only exciting, it's life-changing!

Identity Theft

"The thief comes only to steal and kill and destroy;
I have come that they may have life,
and have it to the full."

—JOHN 10:10

According to the Federal Trade Commission, about nineteen people have their identities stolen every minute. Probably you've heard victims interviewed on the news, telling horrible tales of having to spend thousands of dollars and hundreds of hours to recover lost wealth and restore a good name.

In one sense, identity theft is a new phenomenon. In another sense, it is as old as the human race. The Bible shows God giving people a priceless identity: beloved image bearers created for his glory. According to Jesus, however, there's a villain in this divine drama, a thief who comes "only to steal and kill and destroy."

This thief is the devil. Using lies (Genesis 3:4; John 8:44) and accusations (Revelation 12:10), he desires to blind people to God's truth (2 Corinthians 4:4).

Though Satan's desire is to "take away" the truth we've been given (Mark 4:15), God wants us in his Word—and his Word in us—so that we grasp who we are *in Christ*.

For Reflection

What are some of the lies you've believed about yourself? What lies hold you back from enjoying freedom as one bearing God's image? What are some ways you can let go of those lies?

Prayer

Lord Jesus, I want the life you offer. Protect me today from the thief of truth. Amen.

For Further Study

John 8:31–47

Jesus' enemies argue with him over whose children they are. In response, Jesus explains how the truth he gives can truly set a person free.

Who Am I?

"Open my eyes that I may see wonderful things in your law."

—Psalm 119:18

Think of the hats you wear in a given day. Maybe you're a *spouse* and a *parent*. Don't forget:

- Child (perhaps of aging parents)
- Sibling
- Employee or boss
- Friend
- Neighbor
- Homeowner
- Pet owner
- Citizen
- Taxpayer
- Club member
- Hobbyist

And so on.

Whew! No wonder we get so weary! We wear a *lot* of hats!

But that's precisely the point. Those are only hats. They're *roles*—important ones, to be sure—but still just roles. Those are things we *do*, which is a very different matter from who we *are*.

For many, the question that causes more confusion than any other is *Who am I?* Many individuals, perhaps even you, are in the midst of a full-fledged identity crisis!

Guess what? God doesn't want us in the dark. He's the God who speaks, the God who reveals. His Word contains "wonderful things" that we desperately need to see and embrace. That's the reason for this book.

We need God's help to see the truth of who we are.

For Reflection

What are some reasons it is good to see ourselves in a different way—in the way God sees us?

Prayer

Heavenly Father, as I continue this study of identity, open my eyes to see who I truly am. Amen.

For Further Study

Romans 6:4–14

The apostle Paul discusses what it means to be alive to God in Christ.

Running from Who We Are

"The man and his wife heard the sound of the LORD God as he was walking in the garden in the cool of the day, and they hid from the LORD God among the trees of the garden."

—GENESIS 3:8

I magine being in the federal government's witness protection program:

- Moving to some strange place where you don't know a soul

- Living under an assumed name

- Pretending to be someone you're not

- Forever looking over your shoulder

Talk about a lonely, nerve-wracking existence!

In a sense that's a snapshot of humanity. Adam and Eve had a perfect life in Eden. But sin rose up in their hearts and ruined everything. After they were forced to leave in a hurry, they parented a whole race who were expert at hiding and pretending.

We've been running so long, life in Paradise now seems like a faint dream. And life in an uncertain world makes us feel restless and on edge. What can we do?

The good news is that we are being pursued by the one who knows exactly who we are, loves us unconditionally, and offers ultimate protection.

For Reflection

What are some of the things about yourself that you try to run from? What have you been trying to hide from others? From God?

Prayer

Lord, if I run today, may it be to you. Amen.

For Further Study

Psalm 139:1–12

The psalmist describes the futility of trying to hide from God.

What's in a Name?

"A good name is more desirable than great riches;
to be esteemed is better than silver or gold."

—PROVERBS 22:1

What's the first thing we do when meeting someone new? Easy. We exchange names.

Names are the most basic form of identification. They designate who we are and differentiate us from everyone and everything we are not (e.g., Winston Churchill, Toyota Camry, Miami Beach).

Names may reveal something of a person's heritage. For example, Sean O'Grady is probably of Irish descent and John D. Rockefeller V is probably from a long line of prestigious men.

But ultimately, a name comes to stand for a person's overall character and life. Contrast the ways people react to the names *Helen Keller* and *Adolph Hitler*.

In the Bible, names not only provide identity, they carry authority. For example, doing something "in the name of Jesus" means doing that thing exactly as Christ would do it. Frequently, names in Scripture are changed to suggest a new destiny or a transformation in character.

The Word of God calls the people of God a host of really good names—we are far richer than we can imagine!

For Reflection

What does your name say about you? If you could choose a name for yourself, what would that name be? Why?

Prayer

Almighty God, giver of life, grant me the faith today to believe I am exactly who you say I am. Amen.

For Further Study

Isaiah 43:1–7

God speaks about knowing his people by name and knowing them intimately.

A Case of Mistaken Identity

"This is what the Lord says: 'Let not the wise boast of their wisdom or the strong boast of their strength or the rich boast of their riches, but let the one who boasts boast about this: that they have the understanding to know me, that I am the Lord, who exercises kindness, justice and righteousness on earth, for in these I delight,' declares the Lord."

—Jeremiah 9:23–24

Like us, the ancient people of God got confused about where to find meaning, significance, and satisfaction in life. It took a bold prophet, Jeremiah, to remind them that life is rooted in something much deeper than smarts, power, or wealth. All those things can be lost. True identity and security are found in being a person who knows the Lord.

Stop thinking you are merely a composite of your:

- Job title
- GPA
- Professional resume
- Awards
- Looks
- Net worth

And so on.

Instead, see yourself through the lens of your relationship with God.

For Reflection

Make a list of the blessings God has given you that are yours eternally.

Prayer

God, I am not my successes. Let me enjoy—but not glory in—such things. I'm also not my failures. Please keep me from despair. Grant that I might root my identity in you. Amen.

For Further Study

2 Corinthians 10:13–18

The apostle Paul describes the proper limits of boasting.

"Can I See Some ID?"

"Job got up and tore his robe and shaved his head. Then he fell to the ground in worship and said: 'Naked I came from my mother's womb, and naked I will depart. The LORD gave and the LORD has taken away; may the name of the LORD be praised.'"

—JOB 1:20–21

Though Job's story is primarily about the universal dilemma of suffering, his statement here says something important about the issue of identity.

We come into this world with our birthday suits. That's it—no possessions, no abilities, nothing. Though we spend our lives acquiring stuff and doing things, eventually we *depart*, leaving it all behind. In a real sense, we're naked again. It's just us. Clearly, then, identity has nothing to do with amassing a financial portfolio or building a resume.

Interesting, isn't it? Even when he was overwhelmed with grief, Job recognized that the Lord is where we must look for ultimate meaning and identity.

For Reflection

If we root our identity in our marriage, our kids, our job, or our ability, what happens if or when we lose those things?

Prayer

Lord, keep me from the curse of trying to find my identity in anything but you. Amen.

For Further Study

1 Chronicles 29:10–20

David prays on behalf of the people of Israel, acknowledging that everything they've just contributed for the construction of the temple was first given to them by God.

Why Identity Matters

*"As a prisoner for the Lord, then, I urge you to live
a life worthy of the calling you have received."*

—Ephesians 4:1

Written from a prison in Rome, Paul's letter to the church at Ephesus is such a goldmine of truth, it's easy to miss the significant lesson about identity that its *layout* teaches.

Seriously, notice the way the letter is organized. The first half focuses on eternal truth; the second half on everyday life:

- Ephesians 1–3 ask the "What?" question: What is true of those who are *in Christ*?

- Ephesians 4–6 wrestle with the "How?" question: How should people live once they are *in Christ*?

Grab your Bible and see for yourself. Paul doesn't urge Christians to do anything until he delineates all that *Christ* has done for us. This explains why we don't find a single command until the first verse of the fourth chapter!

The very structure of this letter is a powerful reminder that our deep beliefs about *who* we are will always dictate *how* we live.

Your understanding of your calling inevitably determines your conduct. Your activity flows out of your sense of identity.

For Reflection

Our verse begins with the phrase "as a prisoner for the Lord." How does that description affect the choices you make about what you do?

Prayer

Lord, give me the grace, wisdom, and power to understand and live out the calling I've received. Amen.

For Further Study

Colossians 1:9–14

Paul discusses what it means to live a life worthy of the Lord.

Misidentification

"Trust in the LORD with all your heart and lean not on your own understanding."

—Proverbs 3:5

People and things get misidentified every day. For example:

- That deadly coral snake your son just "dispatched" in the back yard—it was only a harmless scarlet kingsnake!

- You are zero for five this week in calling each of your neighbor's identical twin daughters by the right name!

- The armed robbery suspect who was positively identified yesterday by a convenience store clerk? Evidence discovered today has exonerated him!

Why are we so wrong so often? Because our knowledge is limited and our memories are faulty. And sometimes because we heed the world's advice to *follow your heart*.

This explains how we misidentify ourselves spiritually. Instead of learning—and trusting—what God says, our hearts forget what is true, then whisper, "Here's what *seems* true . . ." No wonder we often call ourselves the wrong names. We effectively kill the truth about who we are, even as we let deadly lies slither around in our hearts and minds!

Understanding who we are will never come from leaning on our own understanding.

For Reflection

Are there times when you find it easy to trust God? Why? Are there times when you find it hard to trust God? Why?

Prayer

Lord, open the eyes of my heart so that I see clearly who I am in you. Amen.

For Further Study

1 Corinthians 1:20–25

Paul explains why divine wisdom is preferable to human wisdom.

Spiritual Amnesia?

"Only be careful, and watch yourselves closely so that you do not forget the things your eyes have seen or let them fade from your heart as long as you live. Teach them to your children and to their children after them."

—Deuteronomy 4:9

Jason Bourne, of book and movie fame, is the fictitious, bad-to-the-bone, top-secret government agent who can do almost anything—except remember who he is. Jason spends his days fighting:

1. for his life; and

2. against a really bad case of amnesia

In a way, the Bourne books and movies imitate real life—at least the spiritual life. We Christians also face a deadly enemy (1 Peter 5:8). And we too have serious memory issues.

This explains why, as our verse says, just before the Israelites entered the Promised Land, Moses gathered the people of God and passionately *reminded* them of God's character, law, and promises—and of their own holy calling.

It's because our natural tendency is to forget what the Bible constantly calls us to remember.

For Reflection

Why do we humans tend to forget God's goodness and the good things God has done for us? What can you do to remind yourself of these things?

Prayer

Father, I am prone to forget what matters most. Help me lodge the truth of who I am *in Christ* deep in my heart. Amen.

For Further Study

Deuteronomy 4:32–40

In his final words to the people of Israel, Moses talks about what God is like.

Namers and Name-Callers

"I heard a loud voice in heaven say: 'Now have come the salvation and the power and the kingdom of our God, and the authority of his Messiah. For the accuser of our brothers and sisters, who accuses them before our God day and night, has been hurled down.'"

—Revelation 12:10

While recounting his astonishing peek into heaven, the apostle John referred to the devil as "the accuser."

It's when we fail that the enemy's accusations become most vicious. Like a skilled ventriloquist, Satan sometimes hurls his hurtful lies through people and situations (Matthew 16:21–23). Maybe you've heard his damning condemnations through someone else's voice.

Why is this so important? Because when we take Satan's name-calling to heart, we think of ourselves as losers, screwups, and worse. In effect, we let him name us.

This is a terrible way to live. In fact, it's no life at all.

A healthy identity requires listening to the voice of the Redeemer, not the accuser.

For Reflection

If it's the accuser who calls us "losers, screwups, and worse," why do we so often cling to these names? What names does God call his people?

Prayer

God, thank you for salvation and for the promise that the accuser "has been hurled down." May your voice resound in my heart above the voice of all others. Amen.

For Further Study

John 15:1, 5, 14–15; Romans 8:17;
1 Corinthians 6:19; 2 Corinthians 5:17

John and Paul share some of the descriptive names God calls the followers of Jesus.

Remember!

*"Remember that you were slaves in Egypt and the
Lord your God redeemed you. That is why I give
you this command today."*

—Deuteronomy 15:15

Someone once described Alzheimer's this way:
Imagine writing all the facts and memories of
a person's life on a giant marker board and
then every day, picking up an eraser and making
a giant sweep across the board. If you have an
afflicted loved one, you know how accurately this
describes the cruel progression of this illness.

There's another kind of memory loss that's even
worse—call it *Alzheimer's of the soul*. Here,
something (or someone) works to erase spiritual
truth and spiritual memories from our hearts and
minds. This is why Moses kept urging the Israelites
to *remember* their identity: "you were slaves," but
"the Lord your God redeemed you."

Biblical remembering is an active, not passive,
exercise. The word *remember* means "to summon
up into the mind." With God's help, we can
remember what's true. For God's glory—and our
own good—we have to.

For Reflection

What Bible verses have you committed to memory? Which verses do you think would most enhance your life if you were to memorize them?

Prayer

Father, may my reading and pondering of the truths in the pages of the Bible keep me from Alzheimer's of the soul. Amen.

For Further Study

Matthew 4:1–11

Jesus is tempted by the devil, and responds in a powerful and intriguing way.

Bestowed or Built?

*"I praise you because I am fearfully and
wonderfully made; your works are wonderful,
I know that full well."*

—Psalm 139:14

While praising God for being all-knowing, omnipresent (everywhere), and all-powerful, David pauses to marvel at his own existence. Notice what he says: He is "made," not self-made. He is the breathtaking handiwork of an infinite, ultimate artist—and we are, too!

Logically, this means we're not blank slates that have to somehow create our own identity. On the contrary, God bestows on each of us a one-of-a-kind identity!

Think of it: Who else, in all of human history, was ever given your DNA, your fingerprints, your personality, your aptitudes and natural abilities, your unique life experiences?

God made you, because he wanted the unique *you*. Now he wants you to glorify him by becoming, *in Christ*, everything he had in mind when he made you.

If you try to be someone else, who will be you?

For Reflection

What are some of the talents, experiences, and qualities that make you unique?

Prayer

God, thank you for making me just the way you did. Help me know better who I am so that I can better help others know who you are. Amen.

For Further Study

Romans 12:3–8

Paul explains how each and every believer has been uniquely gifted to work together with other believers for God's eternal purposes.

Do You Want to Get Well?

"When Jesus saw [the lame man] lying there and learned that he had been in this condition for a long time, he asked him, 'Do you want to get well?'"

—John 5:6

It's one of the most eyebrow-raising exchanges in the Bible. Jesus approaches a disabled man and asks, "Do you want to get well?"

Different people have offered possible explanations for Jesus' disturbing, awkward inquiry. It's either the most insensitive or the most brilliant question ever. Some say the question was Jesus' way of getting the man to realize that change—even wonderfully positive change—is disruptive and difficult. And healing always brings new responsibilities.

Maybe today you feel lost and confused—the very opposite of well. Perhaps you've got a bad case of "Who am I?" syndrome.

If so, Jesus' question to you is "Would you like to get well?" You can make a full recovery, but be forewarned: it'll take humility and study and trust.

When we're sick and tired of trying on assorted identities the way teenage girls try on clothes at the mall, there's one who can heal us.

For Reflection

What physical, emotional, or spiritual healing do you desire for your life?

Prayer

Lord Jesus, I want a healthy identity. Do a healing work in me. Amen.

For Further Study

Isaiah 53:1–6

Centuries before the birth of Jesus, Isaiah writes of the one who will bring ultimate healing.

Let's Start at the Very Beginning

"The fear of the Lᴏʀᴅ is the beginning of knowledge,
but fools despise wisdom and instruction."

—Pʀᴏᴠᴇʀʙs 1:7

As we seek a better grasp of who we are, we'd be wise to ponder the words of John Calvin. A prominent French theologian in the 1500s, Calvin wrote a famous summary of Christian beliefs called the *Institutes of the Christian Religion*. He began his masterwork with these two assertions: "Without knowledge of self, there is no knowledge of God" and "without knowledge of God there is no knowledge of self."

Calvin was essentially arguing that apart from "the fear of the Lᴏʀᴅ" we are lost. This phrase, *the fear of the Lᴏʀᴅ*, refers to reverence for and faith in God. In other words, because we were made by God and for God, only God can tell us who we are. It's when we foolishly refuse to come to God and listen to him that we drift through this world untethered and uncertain about our identity.

We come to know who we are as we come to know who God is.

For Reflection

Pastor and author A. W. Tozer wisely wrote: "What comes into our minds when we think about God is the most important thing about us." What comes into your mind when you think about God?

Prayer

Lord, help me to know you better so that, as a result, I might better know myself. Amen.

For Further Study

Ephesians 1:15–23

Paul prays that the believers in Ephesus might come to know God more intimately.

The Foundation of God's Word

"All Scripture is God-breathed and is useful for teaching, rebuking, correcting and training in righteousness."

—2 Timothy 3:16

Is the Bible just a random collection of outdated spiritual rules written by men? Not according to this passage.

God-breathed (sometimes translated "inspired by God") means God is the source of "all Scripture"— the biblical writings. Working in and through human authors by sparking thoughts and supplying words, God superintended the process so that the finished collaboration (two testaments and sixty-six books total) is *exactly* what God wanted to reveal to the world about himself, about us, and about all spiritual reality.

Inspiration means we can trust the Bible without reservation. When we do, we find it's "useful" for helping us grasp all the truth we need in order to live as God intended.

- Like a mirror, God's Word shows us who we are.

- Like a referee, it tells us when we've gone out-of-bounds.

- Like a foundation and an anchor, it provides stability and security.

For Reflection

When has the Bible been like a mirror, referee, foundation, or anchor for you? Which stories or verses serve these purposes in your life?

Prayer

God, thank you for your inspired Word. Keep me rooted in your truth. Amen.

For Further Study

Psalm 119:10–18

The psalmist recounts the many blessings of reading God's Word.

I Am a Creature

"God created mankind in his own image, in the image of God he created them; male and female he created them."

—Genesis 1:27

Why do we exist? Is the human race an evolutionary fluke? The accidental combination of exactly the right chemicals and natural processes over eons of time?

Genesis 1 and 2 answer that second question with a resounding no. Though short on scientific detail, the Bible declares loudly that humans are the intentional handiwork of a personal God. We're not a cosmic coincidence.

"God created mankind." This fact makes us *creatures*. We exist by the will of another. This means, logically, we're dependent beings. Only God is autonomous and self-determining. Only he, by definition, *has* to exist.

At first blush, this truth is a blow to the human ego. It means we're not independent, much less in charge. We have limitations. But on second thought our creatureliness is encouraging.

The God, who is complete in himself, who didn't have to make you, chose to make you anyway. That obviously means he wants you!

For Reflection

How does the fact that God created you because he wanted you affect your sense of self-worth?

Prayer

God, thank you for making me! What a privilege to be a creature of the perfect Creator! Amen.

For Further Study

Genesis 2:4–25

The Bible begins with the account of God's creation of the human race.

I Am an Image Bearer

"God said, 'Let us make mankind in our image, in our likeness, so that they may rule over the fish in the sea and the birds in the sky, over the livestock and all the wild animals, and over all the creatures that move along the ground.'"

—Genesis 1:26

Saying that humans bear the image of God doesn't mean that God looks like us. But it does mean that we resemble God in some very important ways.

The Greek word for "image" is *eikon*, from which we get our English term *icon*. Icons are likenesses, symbols, or paintings intended to point to the person or thing they represent. This means we are like living portraits, pictures, or models of God himself.

How so? First, like our maker, we have astonishing creative, intellectual, emotional, and moral capacities. Second, we enjoy extraordinary relational abilities. We can know God and other people intimately. We are able to relate to the created world around us in deeply meaningful ways.

The fact that we bear the image of God means we have great dignity and worth—and breathtaking potential.

For Reflection

How does being made in God's image change your perception of yourself? How does it affect your dreams and goals for yourself?

Prayer

God, may I think, speak, and act today in ways that reflect and honor you. Amen.

For Further Study

Romans 8:28–30

Paul speaks of God's goal for Christians—that we might be "conformed to the image" of Christ.

18

I Am a Natural-Born Worshiper

"Be careful, or you will be enticed to turn away and worship other gods and bow down to them."

—Deuteronomy 11:16

Worship, in the most basic sense, is an expression of what we value. In fact, the word *worship* comes from an Old English word *worth-ship*, which means "the state of having worth." Thus, worship is giving our time and energy, attention, and affection to whomever or whatever we consider worthy.

Everyone, even an atheist, worships. All of us instinctively look for something to "Ooh" and "Ah" over, someone to give our allegiance to. We can't not worship.

If God is, as the Bible says, our gloriously perfect, wise, and good Creator, then he's the great treasure of the universe. It makes sense to worship him.

But we don't *have* to. People can choose to worship other things—and we do.

This is the essence of sin: refusing to love and honor the one true God then turning around and giving our hearts to god-substitutes.

As natural-born worshipers, if we don't worship God, we'll find something else to take his place.

For Reflection

On what do you spend the majority of your time, energy, and attention? What does this say you find worthy?

Prayer

Lord, give me the wisdom to see that you are the treasure my heart seeks. Amen.

For Further Study

1 Chronicles 16:23-31 and Psalm 96

King David oversees a joyous time during which Israel celebrates the reasons God alone is worthy of worship.

19

I Am Made to Care for God's Creation

"The Lord God took the man and put him in the Garden of Eden to work it and take care of it."

—Genesis 2:15

The opening chapters of the Bible allow us to peer back through the shadows of history at the world as God originally created it. We see a pristine garden called Eden. We see a solitary man named Adam. We watch God place the man in the garden "to work it and take care of it."

This reveals something important about our identity. First, we are *workers*. Though we grumble and complain incessantly about our jobs, bosses, and coworkers, work is not an inherently bad thing. It's a noble calling. Before sin ever entered the human drama, Adam was working. Work has a glory to it, because God is a worker (John 5:17).

Second, we are *caretakers*. As the pinnacle of creation, we are required to be protectors of God's world. That anger you feel when you see people, corporations, or nations ravaging the earth is because you are a caretaker. We are called to rule over God's creation with wisdom (Genesis 1:26).

For Reflection

In what specific ways could you better care for the world God placed in your care?

Prayer

Lord, help me to treat your world with the utmost respect. Amen.

For Further Study

Colossians 1:15–20

The apostle Paul describes Jesus and his role in creation.

20

I Am Seen

*"The eyes of the L*ORD *are everywhere, keeping watch on the wicked and the good."*

—PROVERBS 15:3

Do you ever get the uneasy feeling that people are watching you?

You *are* being watched! You're *not* filled with paranoia. You're surrounded by surveillance cameras! And think of all the companies that constantly monitor your internet activity! And don't forget the secret government agencies that read emails and eavesdrop on phone calls!

Some people are so creeped out by all this snooping, they "go off the grid." But there's one grid we can't escape: God's. In Scripture, we find almost ninety references to "the eyes of the Lord." The point is that God sees *everything*: "Nothing in all creation is hidden from [him]" (Hebrews 4:13).

If you're up to no good, being seen is the last thing you want. But when you're feeling lonely or forgotten or invisible, cling to the repeated claim of Scripture: you're seen twenty-four/seven by a loving, compassionate Lord.

For Reflection

Is the knowledge of God's watchfulness more of a deterrent from wrong or a calming comfort to you?

Prayer

God, thank you that I'm never, ever out of your sight. You watch me because you care for me. Amen.

For Further Study

2 Chronicles 16:7–9

The Old Testament prophet Hanani discusses how the Lord is ever watchful.

21

I Am Responsible

"Each of us will give an account
of ourselves to God."

—ROMANS 14:12

In a broken world, everyone is a victim of something:

- Bad genes
- Poor parenting
- Family dysfunction
- Systemic poverty
- Racial injustice
- Social ostracism

- Educational disadvantage
- Bullying
- Crime
- Natural disasters
- Illness

We could go on and on.

So why not just surrender to a victim mindset and join the *culture of blame*? Because as human beings we have agency—a fancy way of saying we get to decide how to respond in any given situation. We are free to take action and make changes. Maybe we can't determine outcomes, but we can at least control the choices we make.

This is hugely important because the Bible makes clear that we are responsible for all our decisions, attitudes, and behaviors. This applies not just to those who have charmed lives. It applies to each of us. We're all accountable to God.

The next time life blindsides you, remember you're not a helpless victim. You're responsible to make wise choices and fully capable of doing so.

The fact that we can always respond means we have response-ability.

For Reflection

What are the things or people you have a tendency to blame? How would your life be different if you assumed that responsibility instead?

Prayer

God, keep me from blaming others and playing the victim. I am responsible to you for how I live. Amen.

For Further Study

Galatians 6:1–10

Paul gives the Galatian Christians (and us) important instructions about carrying our own loads.

22

I Am Chosen

"For he chose us in him before the creation of the world to be holy and blameless in his sight."

—EPHESIANS 1:4

How good does it feel to be:

- Selected for the travel team?

- Asked out on a dream date?

- Invited to an elegant party or a fun lunch with friends?

- Given an amazing job offer?

- Accepted into a prestigious college or club?

Let's face it. Being picked feels *awesome*. When a special person or an elite organization selects you . . . well, there's nothing in the world quite like it.

Here's what the gospel says about (and to) each believer *in Christ*: Before time began, Almighty God decided, "I want him!" and "I choose her!" It's hard to say what's more remarkable about this truth—the "Why?" of it or the "Wow!" of it.

To those who say, "Wait a minute. I chose God— not the other way around!" the words of C. S. Lewis are appropriate: "Unless He wanted you, you would not be wanting Him."

Grace means that God always makes the first move.

For Reflection

What do you think is more amazing: the *"Why?"* or the *"Wow!"* of God's choosing you? Why?

Prayer

God, thank you for the stunning truth that you picked me to be holy in your sight. Amen.

For Further Study

1 Peter 2:4–10

Peter describes Jesus as "the living Stone" and the followers of Jesus as "chosen by God."

23

I Am Sought

"The LORD God called to the man,
'Where are you?'"

—GENESIS 3:9

Right after Adam and Eve consumed Eden's forbidden fruit, they heard the Lord approaching.

Stricken by guilt, the fearful couple dived into the nearest clump of bushes, just in time to hear the Almighty call, "Where are you?"

Based on everything that follows in the great story of God, it's clear this divine question was an invitation, not a denunciation.

Over and over, the Scriptures show God pursuing wayward people the way a shepherd searches tirelessly for his lost sheep. Jesus even stated that his mission was "to seek and to save the lost" (Luke 19:10). He comes after us in love.

As author Simon Tugwell wrote, "So long as we imagine it is we who have to look for God, we must often lose heart. But it is the other way about—He is looking for us."

For Reflection

When in your life did you first realize *God is pursuing me*? As you look back now, were there people or events that you now see as evidence of God's seeking you?

Prayer

Father, thank you for the relentless way you seek me. May I never hide from you! Amen.

For Further Study

Luke 19:1–10

Luke tells the story of how Jesus sought out a religious and social outcast.

24

I Am Graced

"Out of his fullness we have all received grace in place of grace already given."

—John 1:16

Tese are good examples of everyday grace:

- At work, you do something really dumb that costs the company a chunk of change. But instead of a reprimand (or a pink slip), the boss takes you to lunch!

- A high school senior flunks an important test three weeks before graduation because "I didn't feel like studying." Inexplicably, the teacher gives him a retake!

What's *grace*? It's undeserved blessing. It's getting what we don't deserve. John says that Jesus gives believers "grace in place of grace." In other words, divine grace is like the waves of the sea—it just keeps coming, washing over us again and again.

Do we sometimes face harsh consequences for our foolish choices? Of course! How else would we learn and grow? But will God ever run out grace for his children? Impossible!

If we didn't do anything to deserve God's favor, we can't do anything to maintain it.

For Reflection

When have you thought that something you did resulted in extra favor from God? Do you ever think you've done something to lose favor with God?

Prayer

God, help me to see you as you are, filled with a desire to give me spiritual and material blessings I really don't deserve. Amen.

For Further Study

1 Corinthians 15:9–11

Paul describes the undeserved grace he receives through Christ.

25

I Am Called

"You also are among those Gentiles who are called to belong to Jesus Christ."

—Romans 1:6

We call in favors, call the kids to supper, get called to jury duty, and wait nervously for sports referees to make calls on controversial plays. We sometimes refer to our profession as our *calling*.

But what about *spiritual calling*? In the Bible, God is described as *calling* his people. In truth, the gospel of Jesus is a call:

- It's a divine summons (2 Thessalonians 2:14).

- It summons us to come out of spiritual darkness and into marvelous light (1 Peter 2:9).

- This marvelous light is the light of God's kingdom (1 Thessalonians 2:12).

- When we respond to this gracious call from God (Galatians 1:15), God calls us his children (1 John 3:1).

- From that point forward, our calling is to be "his holy people" (1 Corinthians 1:2).

How amazing is that? The one true God calls *you*!

For Reflection

Looking at the list above, with which of these aspects of your spiritual calling do you most identify? Why?

Prayer

God, help me grasp that I only cried out to you because you were first calling me. Thank you for your grace. Amen!

For Further Study

2 Thessalonians 2:13–17

Paul encourages believers to stand firm in their calling.

26

I Am Saved

"If you declare with your mouth, 'Jesus is Lord,' and believe in your heart that God raised him from the dead, you will be saved."

—Romans 10:9

The word *saved* in the Bible means "rescued" or "delivered." Sometimes in the Bible, *salvation* is physical—God's people are delivered from enemies, grave illness, or some natural calamity. Much of the time, however, the *salvation* spoken of in the Bible is spiritual in nature.

The reason we need spiritual salvation is because sin both infects and affects us all. Sin is deadly—it separates us from a holy God. We would have no hope whatsoever—except that Jesus came to save us. He made possible our rescue by giving his life to pay the death penalty for sin. Then, having risen from the dead, he offers everyone forgiveness and a new beginning. We need only believe.

As a Christian, you are *saved*. You have been delivered from sin's penalty, you are being delivered from sin's power, and you will be— one day—delivered from sin's very presence!

For Reflection

Who do you know that needs salvation through Jesus? What can you tell this person about your personal experience of salvation?

Prayer

Father, I praise you for your great salvation! Jesus, I thank you for coming to seek and to save the lost. Amen.

For Further Study

John 3:1–21

Jesus explains salvation to the Jewish religious leader Nicodemus.

27

I Am Forgiven

*"In him we have redemption through his blood, the
forgiveness of sins, in accordance with the riches
of God's grace."*

—Ephesians 1:7

For some, guilt is like a ninety-pound backpack they lug through life. Others can't stop looking in their rearview mirror and feeling deep regret over the wrong things they did—or the good things that they failed to do.

If that describes you, read again—and embrace again—the verse above. This is the good news of the gospel of Jesus. "In him we have . . . the forgiveness of sins." Notice it doesn't say "some sins" (depending on their magnitude). Or "certain sins" (depending on when you committed them and under what circumstances). Just "sins." Period. End of story.

Being forgiven by God means you're pardoned. Thanks to Jesus:

- Your sins have been paid for, blotted out, and carried away.

- All charges have been dropped.

- The slate is clean.

- God's not holding *anything* against you.

- You don't have to trudge around under a heavy load of guilt.

Forgiveness means that Jesus took all your guilt upon himself. And set you free.

For Reflection

Are there sins from your past that you still feel guilty about? God has delivered you from those sins—not just the penalty, but the guilt as well. God has forgiven you. Isn't it time to forgive yourself?

Prayer

Lord, thanks for the rich grace of your forgiveness. Amen.

For Further Study

Isaiah 43:18–21, 25–26

The prophet Isaiah describes God's merciful forgiveness.

28

I Am Righteous

"That I may gain Christ and be found in him, not having a righteousness of my own that comes from the law, but that which is through faith in Christ— the righteousness that comes from God on the basis of faith."

—Philippians 3:8–9

What is *righteousness*? In simplest terms, *righteous* means being "right in God's sight." The Bible uses this word to speak of a Christian's eternal spiritual *condition*—having right standing with God through faith *in Christ*. The word also refers to a believer's ongoing *conduct*—engaging in right thoughts and actions.

The gospel insists that we don't earn the label *righteous* by keeping God's law. On the contrary, righteousness "is through faith in Christ." In the miraculous, mysterious exchange that is salvation, Jesus takes upon himself all our unrighteousness, our utter inability to live in ways that please God. He then gives us his perfect standing with God, along with new power to live in right ways.

When we are "found in him"—*in Christ*—God sees us as he sees Jesus: absolutely righteous!

For Reflection

On a scale from one to ten, with one being "completely wrong" and ten being "completely right," where would you put yourself when it comes to how righteous you feel right now? What factors play into how you scored yourself?

Prayer

God, thank you that righteousness comes through faith *in Christ*, not anything I do. Now that I *am* right with you, grant me the power to *live* in a right manner. Amen.

For Further Study

Romans 4

Paul discusses Abraham's right standing before God and whether he achieved that through good works or faith.

29

I Am Reconciled with God

"For if, while we were God's enemies, we were reconciled to him through the death of his Son, how much more, having been reconciled, shall we be saved through his life!"

—ROMANS 5:10

"**P**eople are basically good."

Millions both think this and say this. Unfortunately, it's not what the Bible teaches. Maybe C. S. Lewis put it best when he observed in Mere Christianity, "Fallen man is not simply an imperfect creature who needs improvement: he is a rebel who needs to lay down his arms."

This echoes the declaration of Scripture that humanity is, to put it bluntly, sinful (Romans 3:23). We're rebels. Apart from Christ, we are, in the words of the verse above, "God's enemies." That's humbling, not exactly comforting, news.

Thankfully, the gospel announces the truth that Jesus' death makes a way for us to be reconciled to God! Reconciliation is the act of repairing or restoring a shattered relationship. It's exchanging hostility for friendship.

We are able to enjoy reconciliation with God only because Jesus was willing to endure separation from God.

For Reflection

Is there anyone in your life with whom you would like to be reconciled? Considering how far Christ was willing to go to reconcile us to God, how far are you willing to go to find reconciliation in your relationships?

Prayer

Lord Jesus, thank you for dying for me. Today, help me to live for you. Amen.

For Further Study

2 Corinthians 5:14–21

Paul writes to the church in Corinth about sharing the good news of how people can be reconciled to God through Christ.

30

I Am Ransomed

"The Son of Man did not come to be served, but to serve, and to give his life as a ransom for many."

—MATTHEW 20:28

I f you've seen many action movies or watched enough news reports, you know what a ransom is.

A person is kidnapped and then held as a prisoner until someone steps forward to pay a price—often very steep—to purchase the captive's freedom. The price that's paid to secure a captive's freedom is called a *ransom*. The Bible says that Jesus came and "died as a ransom" for sinners (Hebrews 9:15).

Bible scholars enjoy debating the question: To whom did Jesus pay this ransom price? Some say the devil. Others say God. Still others say it was done to satisfy the cosmic standards of justice.

Such theological discussions are fine and good, but here's the bottom line: When we were captured by sin and staring death in the face, God paid an unthinkable price to secure our freedom. He loved us so much, "he gave his one and only Son" (John 3:16).

God paid a king's ransom for you—meaning you are precious, not worthless, in his sight.

For Reflection

What images come to mind when you think of a ransom? With these images in mind, how does that affect how you think of Christ's sacrifice for you?

Prayer

Lord Jesus, may I never get over the fact that you gave your life as a ransom for me. Amen.

For Further Study

Hebrews 9:11–28

This passage speaks of how the blood of Christ paid for sin and satisfied divine justice.

31

I Am Redeemed

*"For you know that it was not with perishable things
such as silver or gold that you were redeemed from
the empty way of life handed down to you from your
ancestors, but with the precious blood of Christ,
a lamb without blemish or defect."*

—1 PETER 1:18–19

A friend gives you a gift card. You go online, enter the code from the card, and instantly you are able to buy merchandise that was previously "locked up" and inaccessible to you.

This is a good picture of the biblical practice of *redemption*. In the Bible, people who had been locked up or enslaved were set free from bondage when someone stepped forward and paid the ransom, the required price to set them free.

Redemption always involves an exchange. In the example above, you swapped a gift card for credit; then you gave that credit back to the retailer in exchange for merchandise.

In the case of Christ, he first swapped his glorious life in heaven for a lowly life of service on earth. Then, Jesus relinquished his life in order to redeem us forever from sin and death.

For Reflection

Why would it be difficult to assign a cash value to redemption through Christ?

Prayer

God, thank you for paying the ultimate price to set me free. Amen.

For Further Study

1 Corinthians 6:19–20; Romans 5:17; Galatians 3:13, 4:5; Ephesians 1:7; Colossians 1:18–20; Titus 2:14; 1 Peter 1:14–18; Revelation 5:9–10

Three different apostles, Paul, Peter, and John, describe the benefits of redemption through Christ.

32

I Am Free

"If the Son sets you free, you will be free indeed."

—John 8:36

Maybe you've had some of these experiences:

- Being a stay-at-home mom of small children and finally getting a weekend away
- Paying off your last bit of debt
- Walking out of a terrible, soul-killing job into an exciting new position with a big salary increase
- Kicking a bad habit

Freedom, in any form, is a wonderful thing. But the ultimate freedom that Jesus gives . . . how do we put that into words?

Trusting Jesus is like being found in a prison of darkness, death, and despair and brought into light, life, and hope! When we were incarcerated by sin, Christ liberated us. When we owed a huge debt to God, Jesus paid every last cent.

Understand this: The freedom Jesus gives us isn't merely conceptual. It's actual. Before Christ, we were captive to sin and powerless against it. Now, we are free—and free to tell temptation to take a hike (1 Corinthians 10:13).

Use the liberty you enjoy through Christ today to say no to sin and yes to God.

For Reflection

Is there a sin in your life that you are not willing to say no to? Is there something God wants for you that you are reluctant to say yes to?

Prayer

Jesus, may I live out the lyrics of the old hymn today: "My chains fell off, my heart was free, I rose, went forth, and followed Thee." Amen.

For Further Study

Galatians 5:1, 13–18

Paul encourages believers to remember their freedom and not allow sin to enslave them again.

33

I Am Bought with a Price

"Do you not know that your bodies are temples of the Holy Spirit, who is in you, whom you have received from God? You are not your own; you were bought at a price. Therefore honor God with your bodies."

—1 Corinthians 6:19–20

We looked previously at the gospel announcements that Jesus gave himself as a ransom for us, that he redeemed us. Clearly those realities demonstrate how much God loves us.

But here's something else that flows from those truths: Because the Lord paid handsomely for us, he *owns* us. Notice Paul's words to the Christians in ancient Corinth: "You are not your own; you were bought at a price." In short, we belong to God.

Wait . . . not our own? "Bought"? How can this be? Didn't we just glory in the great truth that we are free?

Being free and belonging to God are not mutually exclusive. Paul wrote in another place, "You have been set free from sin and have become slaves of God" (Romans 6:22).

God bought us so that we might find ultimate freedom in serving him!

For Reflection

Does it feel different for you to think of yourself as a slave of God as opposed to being owned by God? If so, how?

Prayer

Lord, save me from the foolish notion that I can find freedom anywhere but in you. Amen.

For Further Study

Romans 6:16–23

Paul describes what it means that followers of Jesus are slaves to righteousness.

34

I Am Known

"God's solid foundation stands firm, sealed with this
inscription: 'The Lord knows those who are his,'
and, 'Everyone who confesses the name of the
Lord must turn away from wickedness.'"

—2 Timothy 2:19

O n an online dating site, a single guy may
try to show off his good points and at the
same time hide his flaws, demonstrating
two things:

1. Humans want desperately to be known.

2. Humans are terrified of being known.

It's paradoxical, but it's true. Because we are made
in the image of God, we are wired for relationship.
In our humanness, we crave connection with
others. And yet, because of bad experiences and
personal insecurities, we are skittish about taking
off our masks and showing our true selves to
others. Even with God, we struggle being honest.

Such realities make the statement "The Lord knows
those who are his" a life changer. Multiple other
Bible verses echo this truth.

God sees past every façade you erect, every mask
you wear. Everything about you—the good, the
bad, and the ugly—God knows. And he loves you
still. So relax. The pressure's off.

With God, you don't have to pretend to be something you're not. Which is good, because it doesn't work anyway!

For Reflection

What masks are you trying to wear before God?

Prayer

Father, thank you for the truth that I am fully known—and eternally loved—by you. Amen.

For Further Study

John 10:14–27

Jesus likens himself to a good shepherd who knows and cares for his sheep.

35

I Am Justified

"For we maintain that a person is justified by faith apart from the works of the law."

—Romans 3:28

Justified is a legal term. It means "to be declared not guilty of breaking a law." For example, a jury exonerates a woman in the shooting of an intruder, calling her reaction a *justifiable* act of self-defense.

The Bible takes this term *justified* and invests it with marvelous spiritual hope. Hear again the claim of the gospel: Any person who trusts solely *in Christ*—in his perfect life, sacrificial death, and glorious resurrection for sinners—is *justified* by God.

The Almighty declares that person not guilty but righteous—not because of their *works*, but because of their *faith* in the person and works of Jesus.

So many blessings flow out of this truth. No matter how much wrong we've done, heaven's verdict is emphatic: "Not guilty!" No matter how much the enemy accuses us, the slam-dunk case against us has been settled and dismissed.

For Reflection

If the judge of the universe says we're justified, why do we so often walk around feeling guilty?

Prayer

God, thank you for the amazing grace that gives me right standing with you. Amen.

For Further Study

Galatians 2:15–21

Paul explains why justification is only available through faith, and not from our efforts to earn God's approval.

36

I Am Accepted

*"Accept one another, then, just as Christ accepted
you, in order to bring praise to God."*

—Romans 15:7

Rejection comes in ten thousand forms:

- You don't get a bid to be in the sorority.
- You don't win a spot on the team.
- A fiancé tells you, "It's over."
- You are passed over for another applicant.
- After a conflict, your so-called friends inexplicably side against you.

To every follower of Jesus who's been told "You're *not* welcome!" here's a bigger and better truth: Christ accepts you.

The biblical verb *accept* means "to draw to oneself" or "to receive hospitably and warmly." In other words, Jesus doesn't look at us through the peephole, roll his eyes, grudgingly crack open the door, and head back upstairs while mumbling, "Turn out the lights when you're done." No, he runs out into the driveway, greets us with a bear hug, and eagerly invites us to come inside for a great meal and an evening of conversation.

Being accepted by Jesus means he delights in us and dotes on us.

For Reflection

When have you felt rejected? Has a fear of rejection kept you from doing certain things? How can knowing you're fully accepted by Jesus make a difference in these instances?

Prayer

Lord, remind me that your acceptance isn't grudging toleration. It's celebration. Help me to treat others in the same way. Amen.

For Further Study

Romans 14:1–4

Paul urges believers to accept each other despite their different outlooks and perspectives.

37

I Am Spiritually Alive

*"When you were dead in your sins and in the
uncircumcision of your flesh, God made you alive
with Christ. He forgave us all our sins."*

—Colossians 2:13

Do you ever feel dead inside? Or, to borrow a phrase from the book and hit movie *The Princess Bride*, "mostly dead"?

It's easy to get to a place where your soul feels lifeless and numb. Especially in circumstances such as:

- When life gets confusing
- When you're reeling from trials that seem overwhelming
- When you've been burning the proverbial candle at both ends
- When you're stretching yourself physically for long periods of time

And so on.

Sometimes, if you're honest, God seems about as real as the tooth fairy.

Maybe you're in that place now. You can't even fake it. You feel spiritually blah, void of energy, and excited about nothing. It's like your faith has flatlined.

Nevertheless, here's what's true of every follower of Jesus: God made you alive with Christ.

You may not *feel* the life of God animating your heart. You may not *sense* the Spirit present in your life. But he's there, and you are spiritually alive.

Sometimes even the living need a little reviving.

For Reflection

What can you do to pump new life into your spiritual walk? Is there a class or small group you can join at your church? An accountability partner you can reach out to? What action step will you take today?

Prayer

God, thank you for giving me new life *in Christ*. Grant that I might live my life fully and live fully for your glory today. Amen.

For Further Study

Romans 13:11–14

Paul exhorts believers to wake up from their spiritual slumber.

38

I Am a Follower

"'Come, follow me,' Jesus said, 'and I will send you out to fish for people.'"

—MARK 1:17

There's no end to all the following that is possible in our media-saturated culture. You can follow sports on ESPN and breaking news on Fox or CNN—all at the same time! You can follow a friend's vacation on Instagram, and an old classmate's ongoing battle with cancer on Facebook. You can follow favorite bloggers on WordPress and big-name celebrities on Twitter. And the minute anyone posts something you don't like, you can "unfollow" at the click of a button!

Contrast this distracted kind of following with the unflinching call of Jesus to "come, follow me."

Jesus wasn't interested in occasional "clicks" and mindless "likes" from half-hearted disciples. He demanded then—and does now—wholehearted allegiance. Following the Lord means self-denial and a life of sacrifice. Being Christ's disciple means giving up one's life for Christ's sweet sake (Luke 9:23–24). We aren't just called to believe in Jesus, but to be with him and become like him.

A disciple follows Jesus in order to know him and become like him.

For Reflection

How is following Jesus different from following someone on social media? How is it similar?

Prayer

Lord Jesus, give me the grace, courage, and perseverance to follow you with my whole heart. Amen.

For Further Study

Luke 18:18–30

Luke describes an incident in which a rich ruler approached Jesus and asked what he need to do in order to inherit eternal life.

39

I Am a Christian

"So for a whole year Barnabas and Saul met with the church and taught great numbers of people. The disciples were called Christians first at Antioch."

—ACTS 11:26

Why do so many followers of Jesus seem reluctant to admit, "I am a Christian"?

- Is it because they're ashamed of Jesus?

- Is it because un-Christ-like believers and angry non-Christians have given the word such a bad rap?

- Is it because the word no longer has a universally agreed-upon meaning?

Here's the origin of the term: The word *Christ* is the New Testament Greek equivalent of the Old Testament Hebrew word *Messiah*—what the Jewish people call the savior/king that God long ago promised to send.

The *–ian* suffix means "belonging to" or "a member of." Thus, the name given to the disciples of Jesus at Antioch, *Christians*, simply means "those who belong to Christ" or "those who are a part of Christ."

Many unbelievers shake their heads in disgust at the label *Christian*. Our assignment is to live in such a way that they shake their heads in wonder.

For Reflection

What associations do you have for the word *Christian*? Do you identify yourself as a Christian? Why or why not?

Prayer

Jesus, what a privilege to belong to you! May I bring you honor as I live today as a Christian. Amen.

For Further Study

1 Peter 4:12–19

Peter reminds believers that even if we suffer for our belief *in Christ*, we should be proud to bear his name.

40

I Am a Conqueror

"No, in all these things we are more than
conquerors through him who loved us."

—Romans 8:37

Maybe you're coming off some kind of failure or disappointment:

- You didn't get the promotion.
- You couldn't make the relationship work.
- You just lost your nest egg in a "can't miss" investment.

In a culture that worships success—the fittest and best-looking, the richest and smartest—it's easy in such moments to conclude, "I'm a loser."

That may *feel* true. But according to Paul, it isn't. Even in life's worst moments, Christians are *conquerors*, not losers. The word *conqueror* means "one who wins overwhelmingly or experiences complete victory."

How can Paul say such a thing? To be in dire straits, yet sit there mumbling, "I am a conqueror!" Isn't this denial of the worst kind?

Actually, it's truth-telling of the best kind.

Notice that we're conquerors "through him who loved us." Christ's love always defeats evil. It always comes out on top. When everything else is down for the count, love still stands.

We can never be losers when we're loved perfectly by the one who is love.

For Reflection

What has been a recent failure or disappointment in your life? Reevaluate that situation from the standpoint of being a conqueror. Does this alter your feelings or perceptions about the situation?

Prayer

Lord Jesus, open my eyes today. Let me see myself—and my failures—through the lens of your love. Amen.

For Further Study

Romans 8:31–39

Paul writes about our standing as conquerors through Christ.

I Am Going to Live Forever

"Now this is eternal life: that they know you,
the only true God, and Jesus Christ,
whom you have sent."

—John 17:3

Many people think of *eternal life* as an abstract, impersonal thing:

- A divine guarantee for Christians, a glorious promise we receive the moment we die

- Another way to speak of heaven or the hereafter

- A perfected, endless version of life on earth

According to Jesus, all these explanations fall short. That's because they fail to point out that *he* is the very essence and source of life that never ends (John 5:24; 6:47; 14:6). Eternal life is a person (Christ), not a place! We enter into *eternal life* when we come to know Jesus by faith.

Consider: If faith places us "in Christ Jesus" (Romans 6:11) and makes us "united with the Lord" (1 Corinthians 6:17), how could we ever die?

We know we will live forever because we are now joined to the one who is eternal life.

For Reflection

Does the idea that *eternal life* is not a place change how you feel about God's gift of eternal life?
If so, how?

Prayer

Lord Jesus, you are the source and supplier of life. In truth, you are life itself. Thank you for drawing me to you and promising that I will never truly die. Amen.

For Further Study

Psalm 39:1–7

King David remembers the fleeting nature of this life, and expresses hope in the Lord.

42

I Am Healed

"'He himself bore our sins' in his body on the cross, so that we might die to sins and live for righteousness; 'by his wounds you have been healed.'"

—1 Peter 2:24

Healing is a major theme in Scripture. The Bible frequently tells of prophets and apostles healing those who suffered with various diseases and physical disabilities. And of course, Jesus, who came to show us God's heart, frequently touched the sick, supernaturally restoring them to health.

Interestingly, throughout the book of John, these miracles are called *signs*. In other words, they pointed to something else, something more glorious. What could be better than being cured of a deadly disease?

This: Finding ultimate, eternal, *spiritual* healing *in Christ*.

When God miraculously cures a malignant brain tumor, we rejoice and rightly so! However, this deliverance doesn't mean our loved one won't eventually die of some other ailment. Barring the return of Jesus, we each have an appointment with death.

The gospel tells us that when sin ravaged our souls like the most aggressive form of stage-four cancer, Jesus took our sickness upon himself and gave us his perfect health.

For Reflection

List the similarities between sin and stage-four cancer. What are the differences?

Prayer

Lord, thank you for the physical health I enjoy—but even more for healing my sin-sick heart! Amen.

For Further Study

Isaiah 53

The prophet Isaiah describes how we would be healed through Christ's suffering.

43

I Am a Servant of God

*"His master replied, 'Well done, good and faithful
servant! You have been faithful with a few things;
I will put you in charge of many things. Come and
share your master's happiness!'"*

—Matthew 25:21

All those New Testament references to
servants and/or *slaves* make us cringe. We
wonder, "Why doesn't Scripture condemn
such a practice?"

It's a fair question, answered in part by the truth
that slavery in New Testament times had nothing to
do with race, and it was rarely long-term. In truth, it
was typically a voluntary economic arrangement—
like what we might label *indentured servitude*.
About one-third of those living in the Roman
Empire agreed to become slaves or servants!

Jesus and the apostles took this common
institution and invested it with spiritual meaning.
By faith—and willingly—we are "servants of God"
and "slaves of Christ" (2 Corinthians 6:4, Ephesians
6:6). In Jesus we find a righteous and good
master who took "the very nature of a servant"
and "humbled himself by becoming obedient to
death—even death on a cross!" (Philippians 2:7–8).

So you see, it's when we humbly live as servants
that we're most like Jesus.

For Reflection

How does living humbly like a servant make us more like Jesus?

Prayer

Jesus, I want to serve you as you have served me— with my very life. Amen.

For Further Study

John 13:1–17

John describes how Jesus washed the feet of his disciples.

44

I Am a Steward

"Each of you should use whatever gift you have received to serve others, as faithful stewards of God's grace in its various forms."

—1 Peter 4:10

In ancient times, the wealthy often had multiple servants. Typically, the most capable and trustworthy servant of an estate would be given the title *steward*. He was then given charge of all the master's possessions, and it was his responsibility to care for those resources and supply them to family members or fellow servants as needed.

Using this custom as an illustration, Peter calls all Christ's believers *stewards*. It's a reminder that God has entrusted us with so much:

- Life
- The truth of the gospel
- Material resources
- Spiritual gifts
- Sovereign opportunities

All are given with the intention that we would make a difference in the lives of others.

When we live as stewards, we share whatever God has put in our care in order to bless others and bring him honor.

We are stewards—managers and conduits—of God's amazing grace!

For Reflection

Think of it: you have a chance today to dispense the grace of God to a grace-less world! Will you? How?

Prayer

Lord, what an honor to be able to serve you by serving others today. Make me faithful. Amen.

For Further Study

Matthew 25:14–30

Jesus tells a memorable story:
the Parable of the Talents.

45

I Am a Disciple

"When morning came, he called his disciples to him and chose twelve of them, whom he also designated apostles."

—LUKE 6:13

When people speak of a young coach having been the *disciple* of an older coach, what do they mean? They mean the one apprenticed under the other. While on his staff, the novice coach was shaped and trained by the experienced coach. The "student" learned coaching techniques and philosophy from the "master"—and likely picked up some of his mannerisms along the way.

This is essentially what the Gospels mean when they refer to the disciples of Jesus. Like eager-beaver students, these men—and quite a few women, which was unheard of in ancient culture—followed Christ everywhere, watching, listening, absorbing. In time, these devoted disciples came to resemble Jesus (Acts 4:13) and were commissioned to go all over the world and make other disciples (Matthew 28:18–20).

Only some believers are called and enabled by God to be apostles, prophets, and pastors. But every believer can become a faithful follower and diligent student of Jesus.

Jesus is calling you to be a disciple-making disciple.

For Reflection

What are you actively doing to become the disciple-making disciple Christ called you to be?

Prayer

Lord Jesus, grant that I might learn all that you are teaching me today. Amen.

For Further Study

Romans 10:9–15

The apostle Paul encourages believers to go and tell others about Christ.

46

I Am Loved

"God demonstrates his own love for us in this:
While we were still sinners, Christ died for us."

—Romans 5:8

After three decades as a marriage counselor, Dr. Gary Chapman identified five primary ways people both experience and express love. He listed these "love languages" as:

- Words of affirmation
- Quality time
- Acts of service
- Physical touch
- Gifts

What's fascinating is that God communicates his love to us in these same five ways:

- God's written word, the Bible, and living word, Jesus, repeatedly affirm how much he loves us (John 13:34; John 15:12).

- Through the Spirit and via prayer, we can enjoy continuous quality time in God's presence (Romans 5:5; 1 Thessalonians 5:17).

- In Christ's sacrificial service and tender acts of compassion, we see love vividly displayed (1 John 3:16).

- What about physical touch? Jesus shows us this love through other believers, who are his flesh and blood body on earth (1 John 4:19, Romans 16:16).

- Ultimately, through the staggering gift of his Son and countless lesser blessings, God's love becomes undeniable (John 3:16, James 1:17).

Perhaps the author Brennan Manning said it best: "Define yourself radically as one beloved by God. This is the true self. Every other identity is illusion."

For Reflection

Which of the five love languages is your favorite way to experience love? Express love? What can you do to experience more of God's love through this love language? What can you do to share God's love through this love language?

Prayer

Lord, enable me to know and trust your love so that I can share it with the world. Amen.

For Further Study

Deuteronomy 7:6–9

Moses describes how God's love lasts throughout the generations.

47

I Am Cared For

"My God will meet all your needs according to the riches of his glory in Christ Jesus."

—Philippians 4:19

Take a few moments to do this quick exercise:

- Make a list of the things you and your loved ones need right now. Be sure to distinguish between needs and wants. Think also of a broad range of needs—financial, emotional, spiritual, relational, etc.

- Next, write down five words that best describe how you would feel if it were completely up to you to supply all those needs for all those people.

In this familiar verse, Paul thanks the Philippians for supporting him financially and also reminds them that God is the ultimate provider. He may provide through a job. Or he may provide through generous people.

But whatever the means, the promise to believers is that our good Father will meet "all" our needs. Knowing this frees us from worry. What's more, it frees us to be generous, knowing we can't out-give God.

When you have a legitimate need, you also have the assurance that God will meet it.

For Reflection

In what ways can you choose to handle your money differently, knowing that God will provide for your needs?

Prayer

God, bless your name! You always care for me. Amen.

For Further Study

Matthew 6:25–34

Jesus explains why we never need to worry.

48

I Am Born of God

"Yet to all who did receive him, to those who believed in his name, he gave the right to become children of God—children born not of natural descent, nor of human decision or a husband's will, but born of God."

—John 1:12–13

Is there a bigger miracle or greater mystery than birth? Every mom, dad, and obstetrician can testify that a birth is excruciating and exhilarating, beautiful and messy—all at once.

Physical birth is a wonderful illustration of spiritual birth. Babies are made; they don't make themselves—same with believers. At first faith is microscopic and embryonic. But like a fetus in a womb, it grows over time. One day all is dark. Then suddenly . . . it's not. You come into the light.

Welcome to God's family! The only thing better than life is new life *in Christ*.

For Reflection

What are the characteristics of the relationship between a parent and a child? Is this what people normally think of when they think of God's relationship to people?

Prayer

God, thank you for saving me and making me your child. Amen.

For Further Study

Galatians 3:23–4:7

Paul describes Christ followers as the children of God.

49

I Am a New Creature

*"If anyone is in Christ, the new creation has come:
The old has gone, the new is here!"*

—2 Corinthians 5:17

New is one of our culture's favorite words. It must be, or advertisers wouldn't use it constantly in marketing campaigns.

What's not to love about new things?

- That adorable newborn baby
- That new car smell
- That classy new café on the corner
- That cute, mysterious new student in your English Lit class

Here's the astonishing claim of Scripture: when you are *in Christ*—that is, when you trust him to make you right with God—you become a "new creation." Your old life is no more. Your old identity as a spiritually dead, hard-hearted enemy of God is gone.

Suddenly you have a new identity and new standing with God. You have a new heart that's responsive to him. You're filled with new life and you've been given a new mission in life—as well as new power to pull it off.

If you don't *feel* new today, no worries: when Christ is your Savior, you are new in all the ways that count.

For Reflection

What do you find most comforting about the idea that you are a new creation *in Christ*? That your past is gone? That you have new gifts and abilities? Something else?

Prayer

God, grant that I might trust your Word's declaration that I am a new creature *in Christ*. Amen!

For Further Study

Ephesians 4:17–24

Paul describes life as a new creation *in Christ*.

50

I Am Rich

*"My goal is that they may be encouraged in heart
and united in love, so that they may have the full
riches of complete understanding, in order that
they may know the mystery of God, namely,
Christ, in whom are hidden all the treasures
of wisdom and knowledge."*

—Colossians 2:2–3

The Bible says much about *material wealth*.
We're told:

- Money is a *blessing*—not a guarantee to
  every believer (Proverbs 10:22).

- It's a *tool* with which we can bless others
  (1 Timothy 6:17–18).

- It can be a *danger* to our souls
  (1 Timothy 6:10).

Consequently, when dealing with finances,
believers are called to be immensely thankful,
extremely generous, and especially careful.

The Bible says even more about *spiritual wealth*.
God is said to be *rich* in:

- Grace (Ephesians 1:7)

- Mercy (Ephesians 2:4)

- Kindness and patience (Romans 2:4)

- Wisdom and knowledge (Romans 11:33)

All these "boundless riches" are *in Christ* (Ephesians 3:8), meaning we may not be wealthy in a worldly sense, but we are spiritual trillionaires!

Jesus came to share the infinite spiritual wealth of God with those who put their trust in him.

For Reflection

How would you answer a child who asks, "What are 'spiritual riches'?"

Prayer

God, teach me how to access the vast spiritual treasures that are mine *in Christ*. Amen.

For Further Study

Psalm 19:7–10

David writes about God's law being more precious than gold.

51

I Am Adopted of God

*"The Spirit you received does not make you slaves,
so that you live in fear again; rather, the Spirit you
received brought about your adoption to sonship.
And by him we cry, 'Abba, Father.'"*

—Romans 8:15

He was only eight, but Buddy had already endured more heartache than most people five times his age. Abandoned and abused, with a history of getting into trouble—who would want such a worthless, broken boy?

But at a new school, he became fast friends with an older kid. Six months later that boy brought his parents to Buddy's orphanage. With eyes full of love and with words full of tenderness, they asked, "Would you like to come and be part of our family?"

Maybe the only thing more beautiful than *having* a child is *adopting* a child. This is what Jesus did for us! He didn't merely befriend us—that would have been stunning enough—he paved the way for us to be adopted into the family of God!

In Christ, you were selected by God to be his child forever and ever.

For Reflection

Perhaps you know a family (perhaps your own) that has adopted a child. What was the adoption day like? What was your spiritual adoption day like?

Prayer

Abba Father, Jesus, Holy Spirit, thank you for my adoption into your family. I am eternally grateful. Amen.

For Further Study

Ephesians 1:3–14

Paul writes about how God chose believers for adoption into his family.

52

I Am a Child of the Promise

"It is not the children by physical descent who are God's children, but it is the children of the promise who are regarded as Abraham's offspring."

—ROMANS 9:8

On a cloudless night some 4,000 years ago, God came to Abraham in a vision. He told him to peer up into the inky blackness and count the stars. "That's how many children you'll end up having," God said (Genesis 15:5). Somehow the old, childless man believed this amazing promise from God.

The rest of the Old Testament confirms that God keeps his word. Abraham's wife had a miracle child. From this little family, God brought forth a nation. From that nation came a savior named Jesus. Through him, Jews and non-Jews alike are offered, by grace and through faith, membership in the great family of God.

Those *in Christ* are the fulfillment of God's promise to Abraham, the great patriarch of faith. As a believer in Jesus, you were one of those twinkling stars he glimpsed that cloudless night!

It's faith *in Christ* that makes us part of the epic and ancient plan of God.

For Reflection

How does it feel to know you are a child of God's promise to Abraham?

Prayer

God, thank you for making and keeping promises. Thank you for including me in your salvation story. Amen.

For Further Study

Galatians 4:21–31

Paul explains what it means that, by faith, we are Abraham's descendants.

53

I Am Light in a Dark World

"For you were once darkness, but now you are light in the Lord. Live as children of light."

—Ephesians 5:8

Perhaps you know a follower of Jesus who truly seems to glow—and not because he just got back from the beach or because she's pregnant or has a really good make-up consultant.

We're talking radiance. You watch, almost in awe, as this person lives out their faith. Their eyes twinkle. Their lives sparkle.

This theme of bright light and shining lives is found all the way through the Bible:

- When Moses glowed after being in the presence of God (Exodus 34:33–35)

- How fire and radiance often symbolize the very presence of God (Exodus 3:2; 24:17; 2 Chronicles 7:1)

- When Jesus gave three of his disciples a brief glimpse of his heavenly glory—it was like looking at the sun! (Matthew 17:1-2; Mark 9:2-3; Luke 9:28-29)

Now you know why it's possible to be dazzling, to shine for the Lord. The glorious one lives in us!

When Christ fills our hearts and when we open our hearts to the world, we radiate God's light.

For Reflection

Is there anything in your life that is dimming the light? What can you do today to make your light shine brighter?

Prayer

O glorious Lord, shine in and through me today, I pray. Amen.

For Further Study

1 John 1:5–10

The apostle John urges believers to walk in the light with Christ.

54

I Am a Branch

*"I am the vine; you are the branches. If you remain
in me and I in you, you will bear much fruit;
apart from me you can do nothing."*

—JOHN 15:5

You grab your electric hedge clippers and a long extension cord out of your shed. With grim determination, you set to work trimming that overgrown hedge along your long driveway.

With eighteen bushes down and only two to go, you look back to admire your work. As you notice all those severed branches wilting in the sun, you unconsciously lower the still-running hedge trimmer—right onto your extension cord! With a loud *zzztttt*, your unfinished project comes to an abrupt halt!

The dying branches. The powerless trimmer. It's all a reminder of what Jesus told his disciples. Likening himself to a grapevine, Jesus said believers are like branches. As long as we stay connected to him, and draw life and power from him, we bear fruit—without even trying! But apart from him we can't trust, grow, make a difference, or anything else!

As a solitary branch, you can do nothing; connected to Christ, you can do anything he asks.

For Reflection

There are various ways to be connected to Jesus, as a branch is connected to a grapevine. Which is your primary way of staying connected? Which way(s) could you utilize more?

Prayer

Jesus, show me how to remain closely connected to you. Amen.

For Further Study

John 15:1–8

Jesus explains how he is the life-giving vine and we are branches that depend on him for life.

55

I Am Jesus' Friend

"I no longer call you servants, because a servant does not know his master's business. Instead, I have called you friends, for everything that I learned from my Father I have made known to you."

—John 15:15

People often speak of best friends, fast friends, or friends in high places. In Jesus, we get all three.

On the night before he died, Christ gathered his closest followers and poured out his heart. Despite their many failures—including the ones that he knew they'd be guilty of before sunrise—he loved the companionship of these flawed men.

It's hard to picture this moment without getting a lump in your throat or your heart skipping a beat. Jesus showed us that God isn't an angry judge who eagerly smites sinners. He's the ultimate friend.

In Jesus, God offers us the friendship we've been searching for our whole lives.

For Reflection

For you, what are some of the key components of friendship? Are these key components of your relationship with Jesus?

Prayer

Lord, I want to be the kind of friend to you and to others that you are to me. Amen.

For Further Study

John 15:9–17

Jesus talks about what friendship with him looks like.

56

I Am an Exile on Earth

"Dear friends, I urge you, as foreigners and exiles, to abstain from sinful desires, which wage war against your soul."

—1 PETER 2:11

It's often said that followers of Jesus are to be *in* the world but not *of* the world. In other words, since this life is only temporary, we must be careful not to allow worldly values to infiltrate our hearts.

The apostle Peter expressed this truth forcefully by calling first-century Jewish believers who were scattered across Asia Minor "foreigners and exiles." This phrase hearkened back to that period of Jewish history when the Babylonians invaded Jerusalem (586 BC), captured the brightest and best citizens of Judah, and took them back to Babylon.

For some 70 years, these Jews lived as *foreigners and exiles* in a strange land. Though far from home and often mistreated, they were nevertheless called to live holy lives and bless their neighbors (Jeremiah 29). We have that same calling.

We are shortsighted if we forget that we're only here on a short-term basis.

For Reflection

What things of the world are most likely to distract you from your standing as a foreigner and exile?

Prayer

Father, remind me again and again that I'm more a tourist than a resident of earth. Amen.

For Further Study

John 17:6–19

Jesus prays for his disciples.

57

I Am a Citizen of Heaven

*"Our citizenship is in heaven. And we eagerly await
a Savior from there, the Lord Jesus Christ."*

—Philippians 3:20

Although some 815 miles (1,312 kilometers) from Rome, Philippi, located in modern Greece, was a Roman colony. As naturalized Roman citizens, the residents of Philippi enjoyed every benefit enjoyed by those living back in Italy. Paul seized on this political reality to remind believers of our true allegiance.

Have you ever been to an American naturalization ceremony? It's a formal gathering, often at a federal courthouse, in which people from other countries swear allegiance to and become citizens of this country. If you've never attended such an event, at least once in your life you should. Participants gladly, eagerly switch allegiances. You won't believe the smiles, the hugs, all the flag waving. It's quite an exuberant celebration.

In a real way, placing our faith *in Christ* is a kind of super-naturalization ceremony. Every right, blessing, and responsibility of heaven is conferred on us. And all heaven celebrates (Luke 15:7).

No citizenship on earth compares to being a citizen of heaven!

For Reflection

What are the benefits of citizenship in heaven? Which means the most to you?

Prayer

Lord, thank you, thank you, thank you for the blessing of being a member of your kingdom. Amen.

For Further Study

Ephesians 2:19–22

Paul writes about our identity *in Christ*.

58

I Am an Ambassador

"We are therefore Christ's ambassadors, as though God were making his appeal through us. We implore you on Christ's behalf: Be reconciled to God."

—2 Corinthians 5:20

You probably know what an ambassador is. Ambassadors are sent to live in foreign countries and represent the interests of the home country.

The apostle Paul invested this common governmental title with great spiritual meaning when he said, "We are therefore Christ's ambassadors." Think of that. We are called and commissioned by the Lord to establish so-called embassies of heaven everywhere we go (Matthew 28:18–20). We get to announce our king's wonderful offer of peace and friendship to a world that is estranged from him.

It's important to remember that effective ambassadors are both knowledgeable and personable. They are always respectful of those living in the countries they serve in. When interacting with others they are truthful and, of course, diplomatic. Consequently, the best ambassadors are often highly respected and give their home country a good name.

Today as you work among and engage with others, remember you are heaven's emissary to earth!

For Reflection

Where do you serve others as an ambassador? In which spheres of your life do you interact with others who are not members of God's kingdom?

Prayer

Lord, today may I represent you with distinction and honor. Amen.

For Further Study

Luke 14:15–24

Jesus tells a parable of God's kingdom being like a great banquet.

59

I Am Full

"In Christ you have been brought to fullness. He is the head over every power and authority."

—Colossians 2:10

When the apostle Paul heard some believers in Asia Minor (modern-day Turkey) were being enticed to look for spiritual truth and fulfillment apart from Jesus, he knew something needed to be done. So Paul took action. The result is Colossians, a brilliant little letter exalting the supremacy of Christ.

Don't dabble in worldly philosophies or human traditions, Paul urged, because "in Christ all the fullness of the Deity lives in bodily form" (Colossians 2:9). The Greek word translated "fullness" here is *plērōma*, which also means "completion." To paraphrase a popular movie, we might say that Jesus "completes us."

And it gets better. Because we are "in" the one with all this divine fullness, we are "brought to fullness" too. Sharing in his fullness means we're full too.

We can suspend our restless spiritual searching because Christ is everything we'll ever need or want.

For Reflection

Since we are full and complete *in Christ*, what influences sometimes make you yearn for something more? How can you combat those influences?

Prayer

Lord Jesus, may I live fully today, experiencing and enjoying the fullness I have in you. Amen.

For Further Study

Ephesians 3:14–21

Paul prays for the Ephesian Christians.

60

I Am God's Handiwork

"For we are God's handiwork, created in Christ Jesus to do good works, which God prepared in advance for us to do."

—Ephesians 2:10

What is it that you do with great skill and artistry?

- Sculpt or paint?
- Cook or bake?
- Wood carve?
- Write or play music?

Maybe you're saying, "Nah, I'm not the creative type." Really?

- Can you solve computer problems?
- Can you fix or rebuild balky engines?
- Can you find and catch elusive trophy bass?

If those things aren't creative, what is?

The fact is, each of us *is* creative. We have to be: an infinitely creative Creator designed us, and he made us in his image!

Musing on all that God did for us *in Christ*, Paul said this: "We are God's handiwork." The Greek word translated "handiwork" is *poiema*. Our English word *poem* is from this word. In ancient literature, it was used to designate an artistic masterpiece.

How about that? You're not a worthless accident or an uncreative mistake. You are a breathtaking work of art—and God designed you to do breathtaking "good works."

For Reflection

What are some of the good works God has specifically designed you to do? If you don't know or aren't sure, what will you do to find out?

Prayer

Lord, show me today the good works you have in mind for me. Amen.

For Further Study

Psalm 139:13–18, 23–24

David praises God for giving him a unique design and purpose.

61

I Am a Temple of the Holy Spirit

"Do you not know that your bodies are temples of the Holy Spirit, who is in you, whom you have received from God? You are not your own."

—1 Corinthians 6:19

In ancient times, temples were where people went to encounter God or, for some, the gods.

Under God's direction and Moses' leadership, the Jews built a portable worship center—a tent called the tabernacle. Later, Solomon constructed a magnificent temple in Jerusalem. In both cases, when these sanctuaries were dedicated, a radiant cloud descended upon and filled each place. This glorious phenomenon indicated that each place was the dwelling of God.

It's interesting that when the church was born and God poured out his Spirit, "tongues of fire" fell from heaven, not upon a place, but upon individual believers (Acts 2:1–4). This symbolism is important. It signals a major shift in the plan of God. He no longer lives in a special building. He lives in his people!

You are a walking, living temple . . . called to bring God to people and people to God.

For Reflection

If we are the temple of God, are we free to use and abuse our bodies however we want, or does God expect something else? What challenges do such expectations present for you?

Prayer

Lord, shine in and through me today as I take you to the world. Amen.

For Further Study

1 Corinthians 3:9–17

Paul writes more about what it means that Christians are the temple of God.

62

I Am a Member of Christ's Body

"In Christ we, though many, form one body, and each member belongs to all the others."

—ROMANS 12:5

Lots of people—too many, in fact—have had negative church experiences. Perhaps this explains why nowadays so few talk about church *membership*. A growing number of believers have no formal affiliation with a local church. If they seek any kind of regular congregational experience, they use phrases like "I *go* to . . ." or "I *attend* such-and-such church."

The clear teaching of the New Testament is that at salvation, we are baptized spiritually into Christ (1 Corinthians 12:12–13). This means, like it or not, we become *members* of Jesus' worldwide, invisible body. We're joined to all other true believers. Christ didn't save us for a solitary spirituality.

Belonging to a body sometimes means pain. Get a toothache and your whole body will be miserable. But membership is also a wonderful gift. Your mouth can call for an appointment. Your eyes, hands, and feet can get you to the dentist's office.

As a member of Christ's body, you need other believers and they urgently need you.

For Reflection

In what ways could you use help from a fellow believer today? Is there someone to whom you can offer help?

Prayer

Lord, help me to show grace to the other members of your body. Amen.

For Further Study

Ephesians 4:1–16

Paul explains how the whole body of Christ works together to grow in love.

63

I Am in Good Hands

"We know that in all things God works for the good of those who love him, who have been called according to his purpose."

—ROMANS 8:28

Where is God when we suffer?

In 1981, Rabbi Harold Kushner, reeling from the death of his teenaged son, attempted to answer this vexing question in a best-selling book titled *When Bad Things Happen to Good People.* Kushner's conclusion? Maybe God simply isn't powerful enough to eliminate all suffering.

The apostle Paul came to the opposite conclusion. Applying the gospel to a broken, pain-filled world, he declared that, in every situation—even our suffering—God is working "for the good of those who love him."

God isn't weak and helpless. He's the great orchestrator. He's weaving *everything* together. We see now the backside of God's "needlepoint," and it looks like a jumbled mess. When we finally get to see things from the front side, we'll marvel at the purpose and beauty of God's design.

In Christ, we are in the good hands of the God who powerfully turns our pain into blessing.

For Reflection

What pain are you currently experiencing? What do you know about Jesus that can help you trust him to see you through your pain?

Prayer

God, give me grace to trust that you are working in ways I can't see. Amen.

For Further Study

Romans 8:18–30

Paul writes about present suffering and future glory.

64

I Am God's Treasure

"I pray that the eyes of your heart may be enlightened in order that you may know the hope to which he has called you, the riches of his glorious inheritance in his holy people."

—Ephesians 1:18

What do you know about wills, trusts, and estate laws?

If your answer is, "Nothing. I don't have much money, so I don't have much to pass on," fine. But there's one thing you must know about inheritances.

In the opening verses of Ephesians, the apostle Paul gushes about the vast spiritual wealth that comes our way when we are *in Christ*. Then at the end of chapter 1, as his words morph into a prayer, Paul says that God's "holy people" (that's us) are his rich "glorious inheritance."

Read that again. We—not gold coins or valuable stocks or pricey real estate—are the great wealth that God looks forward to most! Now you know why in the Old Testament God called his people "my treasured possession" (Exodus 19:5).

While we are excited about seeing God face to face one day—He is excited about inheriting us!

For Reflection

The whole of creation is God's, yet he considers us treasure. What does this say about where we should place our priorities? Who or what is your treasure?

Prayer

God, I don't understand why you regard me as precious and valuable, but I'm *so* thankful you do! Amen.

For Further Study

Revelation 4

The apostle John shares what he saw when he was given a peek into heaven.

65

I Am Crucified with Christ

"For we know that our old self was crucified with him so that the body ruled by sin might be done away with, that we should no longer be slaves to sin."

—Romans 6:6

Okay, put on your thinking cap, buckle up, and focus: these next few sentences are crucial.

Paul says here that if you're a believer *in Christ*, the spiritually indifferent, lost, rebellious person you used to be was "crucified with" Jesus.

Mull on that for a moment. The declaration here is that in a spiritual—yet very real—way, you were *with* Christ when he hung on the cross. When he was crucified, your old self was too. When Jesus breathed his last, your former life ended.

That means the person you were before you met Christ is dead and gone. That person is no more. This is the best of news. For new life to come, your old life had to be dealt with.

Death is normally a sad experience—but the death of our old selves is cause for celebration!

For Reflection

Are there aspects of your old self that you hold onto—even though they aren't good for you?

Prayer

Jesus, grant that I might understand in an ever-deepening way the wonder of being in you. Amen.

For Further Study

Philippians 3:7–14

Paul expresses his desire to know Christ and to be like him, even in his death.

66

I Am Dead to Sin

"In the same way, count yourselves dead to sin but alive to God in Christ Jesus."

—Romans 6:11

In his eulogy, the brother of the deceased jokes about his sister being a certified chocoholic: "If there was chocolate within half a mile, Margie would sense it—and figure out a way to get to it!" Everybody laughs. It's true—as much as she tried to curtail her urges, Margie could never resist a chocolate treat.

As the funeral procession makes its way to the cemetery, you pass Margie's favorite sweet shop. Suddenly it hits you: *Margie's not craving chocolate anymore.*

This is Paul's idea when he says we are "dead to sin." Because we've been crucified with Christ (see devotional 65), our old selves are dead. The more we "count" this to be true, the more oblivious and impervious we become to the enticements and fleshly urges that formerly ruled our lives.

When temptation calls, we get to answer, "I'm sorry, the person you want is no longer with us."

For Reflection

If we are dead to sin, why do we continue to sin?

Prayer

Lord, teach me how to count myself dead to sin but alive to you! Amen.

For Further Study

Romans 7:4–6

Paul writes that having died to the law, we are free to serve *in Christ*.

67

I Am Rescued

*"For he has rescued us from the dominion
of darkness and brought us into
the kingdom of the Son he loves."*

—Colossians 1:13

I n 2009, an American soldier named Bowe Bergdahl vanished from his post in Afghanistan. The response of the U.S. military was immediate and overwhelming. Jets were scrambled. Rescue teams were dispatched. Every resource imaginable was utilized, and no expense was spared in the desperate attempt to find one missing soldier.

In time, evidence showed that Bergdahl had deserted and been captured by the Taliban. Though he was often confined to a cage in total darkness, the U.S. government worked tirelessly— offering ransoms and ultimately a prisoner swap— to gain his release in 2014.

What a powerful picture of the gospel! When humanity walked away from God, he immediately launched an epic rescue plan culminating in the sending of "the Son he loves." The result? Because of his grace, we experience rescue when we believe.

God saved us from being in the darkness and ruled by evil; we are now in the light and under the authority of God's beloved Son, Jesus.

For Reflection

Make a list of the things from which Christ has rescued you.

Prayer

God, thank you for sparing no expense to search for me and rescue me. Amen.

For Further Study

Romans 7:21–25

Paul writes about the glory of being set free from sin.

68

I Am an Heir of All Creation

"Now if we are children, then we are heirs—heirs of God and co-heirs with Christ, if indeed we share in his sufferings in order that we may also share in his glory."

—Romans 8:17

Talk about rags to riches: a wealthy childless couple adopts an orphan from a third-world country. Suddenly she's living in the lap of luxury and the heir to a multimillion-dollar inheritance!

We feel happy for the girl, but might wistfully wish we were heir to a wealthy relative, too. Here's the truth: You are!

According to the Bible, God not only rescues, forgives, and adopts believers, he also makes us his heirs! That means, if you are a child of God through faith, you are named in his will. The glorious riches that await us in the life to come are more staggering than we can possibly imagine.

What's a few billion dollars here and now when the infinite treasure of God himself awaits us?

For Reflection

While we may be in line to inherit amazing riches in heaven, why do you think God wants our focus to be on more non-materialistic things now?

Prayer

Heavenly Father, such blessings! How good and gracious of you to make me your heir! Amen.

For Further Study

Matthew 5:12, James 1:12, 1 Peter 5:4, Revelation 4:10–11

Rewarded in heaven, we will cast our crowns at the feet of Jesus.

69

I Am a Soldier

*"Join with me in suffering, like a good soldier
of Christ Jesus. No one serving as a soldier gets
entangled in civilian affairs, but rather tries to
please his commanding officer."*

—2 Timothy 2:3–4

Of all the "identities" the Bible gives
Christians, this one of being a soldier
may be one of the most troubling.

We've seen the gruesome images from war-scarred
countries. We know William T. Sherman was right
when he muttered, "War is hell."

Fighting? Suffering? We'd rather chill out and make
nice. But according to the Bible, we don't have that
luxury. Spiritually speaking, we are living in a world
at war.

Elsewhere Paul reminds us:

> Our struggle is not against flesh and blood,
> but against the rulers, against the authorities,
> against the powers of this dark world and
> against the spiritual forces of evil in the
> heavenly realms (Ephesians 6:12).

No need then to fire at hostile atheists on social
media or secular progressives in government.
Instead, we need to arm ourselves (Ephesians 6:13–
18) and use the mighty weapon of prayer to call

in some heavenly airstrikes. Our devastated world needs to be carpet bombed with God's grace and truth.

For Reflection

How can you best equip yourself for a battle "against the powers of this dark world and against the spiritual forces of evil"?

Prayer

Father, give me the love and courage to be "a good soldier of Christ Jesus." Amen.

For Further Study

Ephesians 6:10–20

Paul describes what it means to put on the full armor of God.

70

I Am Safe

"Now it is God who makes both us and you stand firm in Christ. He anointed us, set his seal of ownership on us, and put his Spirit in our hearts as a deposit, guaranteeing what is to come."

—2 Corinthians 1:21–22

Spend a few minutes perusing the latest headlines on the internet, and you may find yourself unconsciously assuming the crash position. Diseases, disasters, deviant behavior, doomsday predictions—what a world! Maybe you're wondering if you're going to make it.

Yes, says Paul in the encouraging passage above. God will make you "stand firm." How can Paul be so sure? Because God anointed every Christian with his Spirit and then "set his seal of ownership on us."

Ancient seals served two purposes:

- They were identifying marks that indicated ownership.
- They provided protection (insuring safe delivery).

Clearly, we are not immune in this crazy world to all physical and/or emotional pain. We will have troubles and hurts, but God has pledged to see us all the way home.

Nothing can thwart God's eternal plans for you.

For Reflection

Do you feel safe, despite the dangers of this world? Why or why not?

Prayer

Holy Spirit, fill me, lead me, and give me renewed confidence that I can stand firm in a dangerous world. Amen.

For Further Study

Psalm 121:3–8

The psalmist rejoices that God will not let his foot slip.

71

I Am a Sheep in God's Flock

"Know that the LORD is God. It is he who made us,
and we are his; we are his people,
the sheep of his pasture."

—PSALM 100:3

Why does the Bible so often compare the people of God to sheep?

There are three reasons, at least:

1. Sheep were highly prized by the ancients for their wool, milk, and meat.

2. Sheep are skittish, vulnerable creatures that, left to themselves, often wander straight into danger. They have been known to follow each other off a cliff!

3. God is the ultimate shepherd. He's forever watchful, fiercely protective, and utterly committed to leading and feeding the flock in his care.

Jesus loved all this sheep imagery:

- He spoke of a shepherd leaving behind his ninety-nine safe sheep to go off in search of the one lamb in trouble (Luke 15:4).

- In the end, he fulfilled his own words: "I am the good shepherd. The good shepherd

lays down his life for the sheep"
(John 10:11).

Be comforted. You are watched, guided, and cared for by a shepherd who gave his life to preserve yours!

For Reflection

Few people aspire to be compared to a sheep. What have you learned about yourself through this comparison?

Prayer

Lord Jesus, thank you for being my Good Shepherd. Help me follow and not stray today. Amen.

For Further Study

Psalm 23

King David explains why it's good to be one of God's sheep.

72

I Am the Salt of the Earth

"You are the salt of the earth. But if the salt loses its saltiness, how can it be made salty again? It is no longer good for anything, except to be thrown out and trampled underfoot."

—MATTHEW 5:13

Salt was a valuable commodity in ancient times.

- Salt was used as seasoning and as a preservative—to cure meat and fish.

- Sometimes soldiers were actually paid in salt. This practice may explain the origin of the saying, "He's not worth his salt!"

- Salt, as anyone knows from scarfing down potato chips, leaves us feeling thirsty.

Probably Jesus was thinking of one or more of these facts when he told his followers, "You are the salt of the earth."

When Christians take this truth to heart and live accordingly:

- We really can make people thirsty for God.

- We can make life better, tastier.

- We can keep the culture of a home, school, office, neighborhood, team, etc., from going in a decadent direction.

God wants his people being salty—in the best sense of the word!

For Reflection

In what ways are you acting as spiritual salt in your home? Workplace or school? Community?

Prayer

Jesus, keep me from losing my saltiness. Grant that I may have an eternal impact for you. Amen.

For Further Study

Matthew 5:13–16

Jesus describes his followers as salt and light.

73

I Am a Holy Person

"To the church of God in Corinth, to those sanctified in Christ Jesus and called to be his holy people, together with all those everywhere who call on the name of our Lord Jesus Christ—their Lord and ours."

—1 Corinthians 1:2

We hear "holy people" and we think of spiritual superheroes—missionaries, monks, nuns, and other pious Christians who *always* display extraordinary faith and who *never* say bad words, not even when someone shuts the car door on their finger.

Such thinking is erroneous. Being a holy person does not mean we are a special breed of believers. We aren't the Navy SEALS of the faith. According to the Bible, all Christians are holy—right now—in the sight of God.

This is not because of anything we have done, but because of what Jesus has done in taking away our sin and giving us his righteousness.

Since we *are* holy people, let's *live* like holy people.

For Reflection

Who do you think of when you think of a holy person? Does this image coincide with the way you think of yourself?

Prayer

Lord, today may there be alignment between who I really am and how I actually act. Amen.

For Further Study

Colossians 1:9–14

Paul prays for God's holy people.

74

I Am … Not Feeling It

"For we live by faith, not by sight."

—2 Corinthians 5:7

We stare at the following descriptive words and phrases based on Scripture:

- Loved by God
- Forgiven
- Adopted
- A citizen of heaven
- God's workmanship
- A friend of Jesus

We read along as authors try to explain these truths in books. We attend church and listen to preachers proclaim them in sermons.

Be honest: do you ever think, "All this *identity stuff* sounds great—but I'm just not feeling it?"

Herein lies one of the great struggles of the spiritual life: Are we going to live by our senses, by what *seems* or *feels* true? Or are we going to live by what God says? Feelings or faith? It comes down to that.

In a letter to the ancient church at Corinth, the apostle Paul issued the reminder that what *is* true and what *looks* true are often two very different things.

Today—and every day—do three things:

1. Review what God says is true.

2. Doubt your doubts.

3. Believe your beliefs.

For Reflection

This devotional begins with a list of six descriptions of Christ followers. With which do you most identify? With which do you least identify?

Prayer

Father, give me the grace and courage to trust you completely, even—and especially—when I can't see you clearly. Amen.

For Further Study

John 20:24–29

John relates an incident in which Jesus appeared to a doubting disciple.

75

I Am Equipped

*"That you, a man of God, may be thoroughly
equipped for every good work."*

—2 TIMOTHY 3:17

Maybe you've heard of the Race Across America? Every year a group of brave (some might say crazy) cyclists peddle furiously for twenty-plus hours a day to traverse three thousand miles in about a week. How in the world do they do it?

In truth, they can only complete the race because each cyclist is trailed by an RV that contains everything imaginable that they might need:

- Supplies
- Spare parts
- Backup bikes
- Medical supplies
- Food

All this plus a team of experts and coaches who are trained to do bike repairs, give massages, whip up nutritious meals, and yell encouraging words.

This is precisely what the apostle Paul meant when he said believers have been "thoroughly equipped." This same word was used in ancient times to speak of a wagon that was outfitted for a long trip or a rescue boat that was furnished with every conceivable item needed to complete a long mission.

In giving us his Word, God has given us the wisdom and warnings, the reminders and insights we need to complete his mission.

For Reflection

What has God equipped you to do? What changes in your life indicate he may be equipping you for something different?

Prayer

God, thank you for supplying everything I need to finish the course and keep the faith. Amen.

For Further Study

2 Timothy 2:20–25

Paul writes about the kind of people God uses.

76

I Am Growing

"Like newborn babies, crave pure spiritual milk, so that by it you may grow up in your salvation."

—1 Peter 2:2

H e might be the son of a king, but he surely doesn't act very dignified:

- Throwing temper tantrums when he doesn't get his way?

- Picking his nose?

- Falling asleep during important functions?

How embarrassing! What kind of behavior is this for one with royal blood?

Of course, we have to remember the little prince is only three years old! Though he's filled with kingly DNA, he has to mature. It will take much training and time for him to grow into his true identity.

Guess what? It works the same way in the spiritual realm. Through the miracle of the new birth, we are members of God's royal family. We are actually and truly the children of the great King of the universe. But just as newborns have to learn to eat, walk, talk, think, etc., so do spiritual infants.

Don't be tough on immature believers—including yourself—who are slowly maturing in the faith. Growing up takes time.

For Reflection

Do you consider yourself a baby believer? A teen? An adult? A senior citizen? If you are a senior citizen, does that mean you're finished growing?

Prayer

Lord, grant that I might grow strong in you, as I drink in your Word. Amen.

For Further Study

1 Corinthians 3:1–3; Hebrews 5:11–14

These two passages discuss the kind of spiritual diet that leads to spiritual growth.

77

I Am on God's Timetable

"That person is like a tree planted by streams of water, which yields its fruit in season and whose leaf does not wither—whatever they do prospers."

—PSALM 1:3

Because it was written by people who lived in agrarian cultures, the Bible is filled with references to seeds and soils and crops.

Here in Psalm 1:3, a person who delights in God's Word is compared to a fruitful tree by a river. This is in sharp contrast with the people described in verse 4. Because they wickedly spurn divine truth they end up like dry, lifeless wheat husks that blow away in the wind following a harvest.

This agricultural metaphor reveals much about the spiritual life. Notice the phrase "which yields its fruit in season." This is a reminder that growth isn't always apparent.

During certain months, fields lie brown and dormant. Trees drop their leaves and appear to be dead. Of course, they're not. They're being readied internally for another season of productivity.

When you don't see obvious growth, be patient— fruitfulness will come in God's perfect time.

For Reflection

Do you see signs of spiritual growth and fruitfulness in your life right now? What specific words or images can you take away from today's devotional to encourage you to keep persevering?

Prayer

God, let me be rooted in the truth of who I am *in Christ* so that I may bear fruit for you according to your timetable. Amen.

For Further Study

Galatians 5:16–25

The apostle Paul discusses the fruit of the Spirit.

78

I Am under Construction

"Being confident of this, that he who began a good work in you will carry it on to completion until the day of Christ Jesus."

—Philippians 1:6

Lying in the dark, you think back over your day:

- You blush at the way you spoke to a coworker.

- You shake your head at how, after praying fervently for courage, you chickened out and didn't say the one thing you really needed to say to a friend.

- You regret succumbing to a sin you thought you'd put behind you years ago.

A question bubbles up: Are you making any progress in the faith?

Don't despair. You're under construction. And God doesn't microwave spiritual maturity. Christlikeness is an epic project that will take the whole of your life.

You'll have spurts of growth and times where it seems like you're going backwards. But though you are fickle, God is faithful. Though you'll have bad days, God never will. His grace is sufficient. His power is readily available.

All beautiful and precious things—oak trees and diamonds and people—are a long time in the making.

For Reflection

In what areas are you growing spiritually? In what areas would you like to see more growth?

Prayer

God, grant that I might view my slow growth through the lens of your love and patience. Amen.

For Further Study

Hebrews 6:1–12

God reveals what it means to grow in spiritual maturity.

79

I Am in Need of Seeing

"Then will the eyes of the blind be opened and the
ears of the deaf unstopped."

—Isaiah 35:5

D o you remember stereograms? "Magic Eye" was one popular version. The trick was to stare at a two-dimensional pattern until you'd finally begin to see a three-dimensional image within it.

Oftentimes, glimpsing eternal truth is like this. We fixate on a Bible verse. We see all the words, but the deeper truth in and behind them eludes us. It's like the truth doesn't even register. We see but not very clearly. Maybe not at all!

Isaiah tells us that God has the power to cause "the eyes of the blind (to) be opened and the ears of the deaf (to be) unstopped." Without light and help from above—apart from the clarity that the Holy Spirit gives—all these identification truths will remain just out of our sight.

In the Gospels, Jesus once healed a blind man— but not instantaneously (Mark 8:22–26). At first, the man's restored vision was quite fuzzy. It took an additional touch to bring everything into clear focus.

In the spiritual life, we can't think or act correctly until we see clearly.

For Reflection

How can we know what we don't know? Is it necessary to identify and fill in the holes in our knowledge, or is it enough for us to accept that we don't understand things fully?

Prayer

O Lord, enlighten the eyes of my heart. Touch me until I see clearly. Amen.

For Further Study

1 Corinthians 13:9–12

Paul encourages believers with the truth that we can only know in part now; however, the time will come when we know fully!

80

I Am in the Good Hands of a Sovereign God

"The Israelites groaned in their slavery and cried out, and their cry for help because of their slavery went up to God. Now Moses was tending the flock of Jethro his father-in-law . . . and he . . . came to Horeb, the mountain of God."

—Exodus 2:23; 3:1

God had promised the Israelites a great life in Canaan. So why were they experiencing brutal slavery in Egypt? Despite crying out to God desperately, there was no relief in sight.

The operative phrase there? "In sight." What the Israelites couldn't see and didn't know was that God *was* at work. Even as they were praying in Egypt, God was about to ambush Moses in Midian and make him the answer to their prayers.

What a beautiful encouragement! At every moment, God *is* working, sovereignly orchestrating ten zillion things. Every now and then, he reveals a small glimpse of what he's up to. Most of the time we have no clue.

In the wise words of author and preacher Charles Spurgeon, "God is too good to be unkind and He is too wise to be mistaken. And when we cannot trace His hand, we must trust His heart."

For Reflection

Are you having trouble seeing God in the midst of your difficulty? Think about times in your past when you felt this same way. Can you now see how God was orchestrating events for his purposes—and for your good?

Prayer

Sovereign Lord, because you are good, I know all will be well—even when I can't see what you're doing. Amen.

For Further Study

Genesis 22:1–19

The writer of Genesis tells of Abraham's radical trust in God.

81

I Am Called to Do My Part

"Therefore, my dear friends, as you have always obeyed—not only in my presence, but now much more in my absence—continue to work out your salvation with fear and trembling, for it is God who works in you to will and to act in order to fulfill his good purpose."

—Philippians 2:12–13

Some believers are spiritually passive. It's like they're waiting for God to zap them with holiness. Meanwhile, other Christians engage frantically in spiritual activities as though growth were entirely up to them. Who's responsible—God or us?

The apostle Paul's answer is both. He tells believers to "work out"—not *for*—"your salvation." We can't earn our salvation through our works, but we must work, wrestle, and labor to understand the gospel and how to live it out. Then Paul reminds us that life change is ultimately due to God's work in us.

The Lord is the author and finisher of our faith. But we have a vital role to play, too. God's part is to patiently stir, reveal, empower, encourage, and transform. Our role is to draw near to God through spiritual disciplines like prayer and to respond to him with faith and obedience.

For Reflection

Are you playing your part in fulfilling God's good purposes for you? For your family? For your church and community?

Prayer

Lord, thank you for working in me as I walk with you. Amen.

For Further Study

2 John 1:1–6

The "Beloved Apostle"—John—encourages believers to love and obey God.

82

I Am in Training

"Have nothing to do with godless myths and old wives' tales; rather, train yourself to be godly."

—1 Timothy 4:7

Writing to his young protégé Timothy, a pastor in Ephesus, the apostle Paul urged, "Train yourself to be godly."

Did you know that the Greek verb translated "train yourself" is where we get our English word *gymnasium*? In effect, Paul was saying, "Hey, Timothy, you need to start working out spiritually! You need to engage in exercises that will strengthen your soul and build godliness into your life!"

He was talking about *spiritual disciplines.* A spiritual discipline is any regular activity that brings us into God's transforming presence:

- Solitude
- Prayer
- Bible study
- Scripture memory
- Serving others
- Worship
- Confession

We develop these holy habits—and others—not to win brownie points with God, but to train our hearts to be more attentive to God and less enamored with the world.

Remembering who you are *in Christ* is a critical exercise in your spiritual-training regimen.

For Reflection

Which of the spiritual disciplines listed above are part of your regular spiritual work out? Which are not?

Prayer

Lord Jesus, keep me from the trap of viewing spiritual disciplines as a "have to." Let me see them as a "get to"—an ingenious way to draw near to you and be transformed. Amen.

For Further Study

1 Corinthians 9:24–27

Paul gives encouragement to believers to run the race of faith.

83

I Am Willing to Change My Mind

"'The time has come,' he said. 'The kingdom of God has come near. Repent and believe the good news!'"

—MARK 1:15

The first command of Jesus in the Gospel of Mark is, "Repent and believe the good news!"

The Greek word *metanoeo*, translated in English as *repent*, literally means "to change the mind." When we add this idea to the Hebrew meaning of "to turn around," we get a beautiful word that conveys the idea of seeing in a clear new way with the result that one begins moving in a better direction.

In repentance, we realize that Jesus *is* who he claims to be—the Son of God, the Savior of the world, the Lord of the universe. Embracing this truth, we turn back. We put our trust in Jesus and follow him.

Repenting and believing is not only the way a person initially comes to Christ; it is also how believers walk with him the rest of their days. As the great reformer John Calvin once observed, "Repentance is not merely the start of the Christian life; it is the Christian life."

Grasping who we truly are *in Christ* requires continual turning back and trusting.

For Reflection

Is there something in your life about which you need "to change your mind"?

Prayer

O God, help me to grow in both repenting and believing. Amen.

For Further Study

Romans 2:1–11

Paul writes about God's righteous judgment.

84

I Am Being Renewed

"I urge you, brothers and sisters, in view of God's mercy, to offer your bodies as a living sacrifice, holy and pleasing to God—this is your true and proper worship. Do not conform to the pattern of this world, but be transformed by the renewing of your mind. Then you will be able to test and approve what God's will is—his good, pleasing and perfect will."

—Romans 12:1–2

Romans 12:1–2 is crucial because it's located between eleven chapters of "here's what God has done for us" and five concluding chapters of "here's how we should respond."

The critical truth found in these hinge verses? Spiritual transformation requires that we let God's truth reshape our thinking.

Paul reminds us here that the world is constantly trying to squeeze us into its way of thinking by giving us an identity that's contrary to what God says is true. If we accept these worldly lies, we'll stumble aimlessly through life, continuing to live in our old ways. But if we'll consistently embrace who God says we are, we can truly renew our minds.

It's as we think in new and true ways, that we are able to live the new and true life of Christ.

For Reflection

Who do you think the world says that you are?
Is that who God says you are in his Word?

Prayer

Lord, strengthen my desire to participate willingly
in your plan to transform my life by renewing my
mind with truth. Amen.

For Further Study

Titus 3:1–8

Paul writes about the role of the Holy Spirit in
God's "renewal plan" for his children.

85

I Am Able to Think Correctly

"Finally, brothers and sisters, whatever is true, whatever is noble, whatever is right, whatever is pure, whatever is lovely, whatever is admirable—if anything is excellent or praiseworthy—think about such things."

—PHILIPPIANS 4:8

We have zero control over most things in life:

- The weather
- What people say about us behind our backs
- How our bosses will react to the bad news we need to share with them
- How our kids behave when they are out of our sight.

One of the few things we *can* control is where we set our minds (Colossians 3:2; Isaiah 26:3). As Paul asserts in the verse above, we can cultivate the habit of focusing on what's pure and true.

Like all habits, this one requires diligent and consistent effort to form. But with God's help, we can learn to think consciously about what we're thinking! And when we find ourselves drifting into pessimism, impurity, or falsehood, we can round up such wrong thoughts (2 Corinthians 10:5) and replace them with uplifting affirmations.

In Christ, we can choose moment by moment to set our minds on what is true and beautiful.

For Reflection

Do you find yourself focusing on the negative in your life? What practical steps can you take today to change that?

Prayer

Lord, show me how to corral my thoughts and channel them in good and godly directions. Amen.

For Further Study

Colossians 3:1–4

Paul urges believers to set our hearts and minds on things above.

86

I Am a Believer

"So then, just as you received Christ Jesus as Lord, continue to live your lives in him."

—Colossians 2:6

We receive Christ by faith (John 1:12). Period. That's the *only* way to come alive spiritually.

This means that when Paul says, "As you received Christ . . . continue to live . . . in him," he means, live by *faith*. Be a *believer*. Trust God—that's our primary job description in life.

This is, as you surely know by now, harder than it sounds. Here's how author Flannery O'Connor described it:

> Faith comes and goes. It rises and falls like the tides of an invisible ocean. If it is presumptuous to think that faith will stay with you forever, it is just as presumptuous to think that unbelief will.

She didn't mean we are *in Christ* one day and lost the next. She meant there will be times when we utterly trust what God says and other days when belief is a titanic struggle. Like the faith-challenged father in Mark 9:24, we'll cry out to God: "I do believe; help me overcome my unbelief!"

You're a believer—so make it your goal today to doubt your doubts and believe your beliefs.

For Reflection

Frederick Buechner said that "doubt is the ants in the pants of faith." Do you agree? How would describe the interaction of faith and doubt in your own words?

Prayer

Lord Jesus, show me how to build my faith and dismantle my doubt. Amen.

For Further Study

Luke 7:18–23

Luke reminds us that even the great John the Baptist had moments of doubt.

87

I Am Merciful

"Be merciful, just as your Father is merciful."

—LUKE 6:36

Without getting permission, a kid takes his big brother's soccer ball to the park. It promptly disappears.

When the boy fearfully and tearfully confesses—with loud promises to replace the lost ball—the big brother replies softly, "No worries. I forgive you."

Mercy.

Jesus mentioned this beautiful quality while teaching on what it looks like to love the way God loves. A *merciful* person demonstrates forgiveness when justified in "letting someone have it." Mercy is pardon, plus heartfelt compassion.

Here's why we bring up mercy in a book about identity *in Christ*: Many believers struggle with perfectionism. They wrongly think they should be doing *everything* exactly right in the spiritual life. Any time they forget truth or fail to live it out, they become extremely self-critical.

It has been pointed out that Jesus' command to "be merciful" needs to apply, not only to the way we treat others, but also to the way we treat ourselves.

If God doesn't berate us when we struggle to grow, why do we beat up ourselves?

For Reflection

Is there an area of struggle in your life? Are you beating yourself up over it? What advice would you give to a dear friend or family member? Give that same loving advice to yourself.

Prayer

Father, thank you for your mercy. Fill me with compassion, so I can be merciful to everyone, including myself. Amen.

For Further Study

Psalm 25:4–7

The psalmist praises God's great mercy.

88

I Am Committed to Integrity

"Because of my integrity you uphold me and set me in your presence forever."

—Psalm 41:12

In the Bible, a person with *integrity* is one who has an upright or blameless character.

One definition of *integrity* is "wholeness." A bridge with structural integrity is safe because *every* pile and girder is in place, the decking is sound, and all those parts are integrated into a strong, stable whole.

The opposite of integrity is *disintegration*. That old wooden bridge that's missing bolts, that has beams that are rotten and disconnected from each other—it's defective. It *looks* stable, but don't dare drive on it!

In Christ, God makes our disintegrated lives whole. A life of integrity isn't perfection. It's steadily finishing the great building project he's already started in our souls.

At the first sign of disrepair, we can call on God to make us as whole in life as we are in truth.

For Reflection

What areas of your life are disintegrating? Write a prayer to God and ask him to make you whole.

Prayer

Lord, you say I am blameless, and for that I praise you. Now help me *display* Christ through a life of integrity. Amen.

For Further Study

Job 2:1–10

Job maintains his integrity despite his troubles.

89

I Am Rewarded for Humility

"But he gives us more grace. That is why Scripture says: 'God opposes the proud but shows favor to the humble.'"

—JAMES 4:6

C. S. Lewis called pride "the great sin," adding that "it was through Pride that the devil became the devil"!

When we're proud, we exalt ourselves. Our heads inflate with arrogance and we start believing the crazy lie that we don't need God or anyone else.

As you grapple with living out your identity *in Christ*, beware of all such spiritual cockiness. Pay attention to James' warning: "God opposes the proud."

Whoa. Being at odds with the Almighty doesn't sound like the path to a satisfying life! But notice what else is true: "God . . . shows favor to the humble."

We demonstrate humility by:

- Admitting we're stuck
- Confessing our failures
- Acknowledging our need for divine help

And when we do, God rushes toward us with a generous helping of his favor in the form of wisdom, forgiveness, power—or whatever we need.

God blesses us, not because we're great, but because he is!

For Reflection

Is there a limit on how much humility we need? How can you cultivate your humility?

Prayer

God, keep me from the great sin of pride so that I might experience and enjoy your generous favor. Amen.

For Further Study

1 Peter 3:8–12

Peter teaches about how the Lord is attentive to the righteous.

90

I Am Strong and Can Endure

"You need to persevere so that when you have done the will of God, you will receive what he has promised."

—Hebrews 10:36

When Kevin started weight training, he could barely bench press 135 pounds once—and then he felt weak the rest of the day! Now, after faithfully working out at least three times a week for the last year, he is able to lift almost twice that weight ten times in a row!

Here is an excellent picture of the power and reward of endurance. *Hupomenó*, the Greek word for *persevere*, is a combination of two words: *hypó*, meaning "under" and *mén*, meaning "remain." This explains how Kevin was able to get so strong. He endured regular, grueling training sessions in which he literally *remained under* a lot of weight. All that pushing and straining gradually increased his power and stamina.

We develop spiritual endurance the same way. We do spiritual exercises like:

- Showing up—solitude and silence
- Opening up—confessing sin and looking into God's Word
- Looking up—prayer and worship

By "remaining under" the truth of God's Word, we become spiritually strong.

For Reflection

Which of the three spiritual exercises described on the previous page will you commit to doing on a regular basis? Begin today!

Prayer

God, keep me from quitting when the spiritual life gets hard. Amen.

For Further Study

Hebrews 12:1–3

The writer of Hebrews exhorts believers to not grow weary and lose heart.

91

I Am Dependent

"I cling to you; your right hand upholds me."

PSALM 63.8

Heart racing, stomach doing somersaults, you stand on the thirty-foot-tall platform, preparing to ride a zip line out across a big ravine.

You just watched dozens of others do this and live to tell the tale. The equipment is new. The instructors are highly competent. Nevertheless, you're terrified.

With a vise-like grip, you clutch the thick rope that attaches you to the zip line above. After a few verbal encouragements—and finally a firm shove—the platform disappears beneath you. Gravity takes over. You're falling. You instinctively pull upward with all your might as you fly above the trees. Only when you're done does it dawn on you that you were holding on for dear life—in vain. It was the strong line and good harness that kept you from falling.

Clinging is good. But David realized a bigger truth: he was held. That's how he was able to trust.

We can depend on our God because he is always dependable.

For Reflection

When in your life have you been most aware of your dependence on God? Have there been times when you were not aware of your dependence on him?

Prayer

God, may the truth that you will never let me go motivate me to *never* let go of you. Amen.

For Further Study

Isaiah 41:8–13

Isaiah reveals how the Lord takes us by the hand and holds us up.

92

I Am Assured

"For no matter how many promises God has made, they are 'Yes' in Christ. And so through him the 'Amen' is spoken by us to the glory of God."

—2 Corinthians 1:20

Depending on the definition you accept, the source you believe, and the counting method you use, there are anywhere from three thousand to five thousand promises in Scripture.

That's a boatload of divine assurances! Even if we go with the lower number, we have ample reasons to live with confidence—even when we face the kinds of difficulties the apostle Paul routinely faced.

Ever since meeting Christ on the Damascus Road (Acts 9:1–19), Paul was laser-focused on Jesus. Paul saw him as the ultimate fulfillment of every promise of God. In Paul's view, when you have Jesus, you have everything.

No wonder Paul said that the more we meditate on the Bible's spiritual certainties—especially assurances about who we are *in Christ*—the more our hearts cry "Amen," which literally means "may it be so."

God keeps every promise he makes.

For Reflection

What are some of the promises that God makes to us in the Bible? Are you relying on those promises?

Prayer

Father, when you say something is so, it is so! Thank you for being trustworthy. Amen.

For Further Study

Hebrews 11:1–13

The Spirit inspires a list of Bible people who acted on faith and relied on God's promises.

93

I Am a Fighter

*"Fight the good fight of the faith. Take hold of
the eternal life to which you were called
when you made your good confession
in the presence of many witnesses."*

—1 Timothy 6:12

Life is a constant battle. About the time all is quiet on the home front, mortar fire breaks out at work. We advance financially only to get driven back by unexpected bills. Every day it's something:

- Relational bombshells
- Missile attacks on our health
- Emotional landmines
- Outflanking maneuvers by our kids

By bedtime lots of days, don't you feel like waving the white flag?

In the realm of faith, it's no different. We're always under siege—which is why Paul urges, "Fight the good fight of the faith."

Today that means you need to "put on the full armor of God, so that you can take your stand against the devil's schemes" (Ephesians 6:11). For part of the day, you may have to dig a foxhole, hunker down, and hold your ground. Later, you may need to find your lost platoon, tend to a wounded comrade in arms, or gather some intel. At some point, you'll need to launch a raid against some sin that's made a prisoner of your heart.

You're a fighter in the great battle of life—but don't despair. You're on the winning side!

For Reflection

What percentage of the time do you feel like you are on the winning side in the battle of life? How would your life be different if you felt that way 100 percent of the time?

Prayer

God, give me strength and renewed perspective as I fight today. Amen.

For Further Study

Psalm 18:37–49

The psalmist exults in how God enables us to fight our enemies.

94

I Am Determined to Remember

Do not merely listen to the word, and so deceive
yourselves. Do what it says. Anyone who listens
to the word but does not do what it says is like
someone who looks at his face in a mirror and,
after looking at himself, goes away and
immediately forgets what he looks like."

—JAMES 1:22–24

"It is my conviction," author John Stott wrote, "that our heavenly Father says the same to us every day: 'My dear child, you must always remember who you are.'"

This is our greatest need. And why? Because our most common tendency is to hear the truth, walk away, and forget what we just heard.

James said that overcoming our tendency to forget requires us to do two things:

1. "Listen to the word."

2. "Do what it says."

So, for example, in the previous devotion, we saw that believers are *fighters*. Don't just nod at that truth. Live it out! Be a fighter today. Attack a sinful habit in your life. Wage spiritual warfare by praying boldly for a friend in trouble.

Determine to be a follower of Jesus who actively remembers their identity *in Christ*.

For Reflection

What symbolic mirror can we look into to see the reflection of who we are *in Christ*? How can we keep from forgetting?

Prayer

Lord Jesus, make me a doer, not a forgetter, of your truth. Amen.

For Further Study

1 Chronicles 16:8–22 and Psalm 105

David praises God by remembering his many favors.

I Am Surrounded
by Saints

*"Therefore encourage one another and build each
other up, just as in fact you are doing."*

—1 Thessalonians 5:11

With genuine humility, the star quarterback accepts the MVP award and then promptly gives the lion's share of credit to his coaches and teammates: "I know it's a cliché to say what I'm about to say, but it's true: Football is about team. Believe me when I tell you I couldn't do what I do if it weren't for the amazing group of people around me."

Every right-thinking Christian with experience in a healthy faith community could give the same speech. We need each other. We weren't meant to live the spiritual life in isolation. That's why the New Testament lists so many ways we need to help each other, assorted things we must do for one another. Encouragement—both gentle consolation when we're struggling and firm admonition when we're straying—is one such way we come alongside each other.

Embracing and living out your true identity *in Christ* goes better when you do it in community.

For Reflection

Are you active in a small group or fellowship class? Do you have an accountability partner? If not, why not commit to one today?

Prayer

Lord, thank you for the power of Christian community. Use it in my life for your purposes. Amen.

For Further Study

Hebrews 10:23–25

God's Word stresses our need to spend time with other believers.

96

I Am a Messenger

"You are a chosen people, a royal priesthood, a holy nation, God's special possession, that you may declare the praises of him who called you out of darkness into his wonderful light."

—1 Peter 2:9

Writing to believers who were scattered and scared—and, in some cases, scarred—from persecution, Peter reviewed who they were *in Christ*: "chosen people, a royal priesthood, a holy nation, God's special possession."

No question this powerful reminder of noble identity boosted their spirits. And yet making his readers *feel better* wasn't Peter's primary goal. Notice the desired outcome of all this great truth: "that you may *declare the praises of him* who called you out of darkness" (emphasis added).

That's huge! We don't read books like this or meditate on who God says we are for *our own benefit*. We use this truth for the glory of God and the good of the world.

The more we perceive the good news of what God has done for and in us, the more we want to proclaim it!

For Reflection

When was the last time you had news so good you couldn't wait to share it with others? Isn't the good news of what Jesus has done for us even better news than that?

Prayer

God, give me an opportunity today as a chosen child of God to share how you have changed my life. Amen.

For Further Study

Acts 5:33–42

Luke records the apostles' determination to never stop telling the good news.

97

I Am Becoming the Person God Created Me to Be

"Grow in the grace and knowledge of our Lord and Savior Jesus Christ. To him be glory both now and forever! Amen."

—2 Peter 3:18

Someone put an eagle egg into the nest of a prairie chicken. The confused eagle grew up scratching about in the dust, eating seeds and worms. One day it asked about the magnificent bird it saw soaring through the blue skies above.

"That's an eagle!" came the reply. "The greatest of all the birds. But we will *never* be like him!" The eagle nodded and resumed pecking in the dirt. He died years later, convinced he was only a prairie chicken.

Sadly, this is the story of many Christians. They haven't a clue as to their true identity. Rather than grow into who God says they are *in Christ*, they settle for far less.

Don't accept what *seems* to you to be true. As Peter says, "Grow!" As the great wizard Gandalf said to skittish little Bilbo in the classic book *The Hobbit*, "There is more to you than you know."

For Reflection

If you believe there is more to you than you know how can this change the way you act? The choices you make?

Prayer

Lord Jesus, help me grow in the grace and knowledge of you, so that I become all you created me to be. Amen.

For Further Study

2 Peter 1:3–11

The apostle Peter discusses growth *in Christ*.

98

I Am Helped by God's Spirit

"I will ask the Father, and he will give you another advocate to help you and be with you forever—the Spirit of truth. The world cannot accept him, because it neither sees him nor knows him. But you know him, for he lives with you and will be in you."

—JOHN 14:16–17

Were you one of those kids who had an invisible friend?

Imagine for a moment a real-life invisible friend:

- As strong as Samson
- As wise as Solomon
- As present as the air you breathe

Let's say this friend knows you inside and out, far better than you know yourself. And let's say this friend can predict every situation you'll ever face and can provide exactly what you need to face the situation.

Would you take an invisible friend like that? You already have one. He's called "the Spirit of truth." He lives inside believers, teaching us, convicting us when we err, and empowering us for service.

It's the indwelling Holy Spirit who guides us into the truth of who we are *in Christ*.

For Reflection

On a scale from one to ten, with one being "never" and ten being "constantly," how aware are you of the presence of the Holy Spirit in your life on a day-to-day basis?

Prayer

Spirit of the living God, reign in me and fill me. Make me more like Jesus, I pray. Amen.

For Further Study

Romans 8:1–17

Paul unpacks what's possible when we live by the Spirit.

99

I Am Granted Anytime Access to God's Throne Room

"Let us then approach God's throne of grace with confidence, so that we may receive mercy and find grace to help us in our time of need."

—Hebrews 4:16

Do you recall the classic scene in *The Wizard of Oz* where Dorothy and her traveling companions entered the hall of "the great and powerful Oz"? They trembled and stammered as they appealed for courage, smarts, heart, and a way home.

Spoiler alert: Little did they know that Oz was *not* a real wizard, and that he had no actual power.

Compare this scene to the invitation in the verse above:

- Because of Christ, believers are given access to "God's throne of grace." In other words, God's not hiding behind some curtain.

- When are we allowed to approach? "In our time of need." The most honest and spiritually aware among us realize that means *all the time.*

- It gets better. We can "approach . . . with confidence." Not irreverently, but also not cowering in fear.

- And unlike Dorothy and her friends with the impotent wizard, when we come to God's throne, we receive the divine help we need.

What better place is there to find grace than at God's throne of grace?

For Reflection

When you talk to God, do you pray with confidence? Confidence that God hears you? Confidence that he cares? Confidence that he will answer?

Prayer

Lord, as I struggle to know and love and follow you, give me sense enough to remain in your presence. Amen.

For Further Study

Hebrews 4:14–16

The writer of Hebrews explains why and how imperfect people can approach the throne of God.

100

I Am …

"Whoever has ears, let them hear what the Spirit says to the churches. To the one who is victorious, I will give some of the hidden manna. I will also give that person a white stone with a new name written on it, known only to the one who receives it."

—Revelation 2:17

Who are we *in Christ*? We are every glorious thing we've talked about in these pages.

And, as if all that weren't enough, we have one additional identity.

Tucked over in the last book of the Bible is the cryptic passage above. No one really knows exactly what it means. "To the one who is victorious" there is the promise of "hidden manna" and "a white stone." And on that white stone is inscribed "a new name."

God only knows the name that will be on your stone. For now, he's keeping it under wraps. When he reveals it—apparently only to you—it will be a kind of endearing heavenly nickname.

For all eternity, God will call you by a name that will fill you with joy.

For Reflection

Who are some of the people in the Bible who received new names from God? How does it feel to know that you are in their number?

Prayer

God, thank you for my true identity *in Christ*. I look forward to being victorious and receiving a new name! Amen.

For Further Study

Philippians 3:17–21

Paul glories in the truth that our true home is in heaven.

Keep your devotional life going strong with these great titles from Hendrickson Rose:

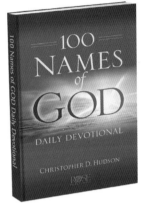

100 Names of God

What's in a name? In God's case, everything! From Elohim (Mighty Creator) and Jehovah Ezrah (My Helper) to Logos (the Word) and Basileus Basileon (King of kings), author Chris Hudson reflects on the meanings of God's titles to reveal his true character—and to encourage you to open your heart to the presence of El Chai (the Living God).

208 pages, padded hardcover
ISBN: 9781628622911
Product Code: 4082X

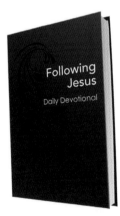

Following Jesus

"Come, follow me." With those three simple words, Jesus called his first disciples to join him on a journey that would forever change their lives. Today, he offers you the same invitation. Each of the 100 daily readings provides a short devotion, a key Bible verse, a reflection question, and a prayer. Strengthen your faith as you move through Scripture toward refreshment and a deeper understanding of what it means to walk every step with Jesus.

208 pages, Flexisoft cover
ISBN: 9781628624021
Product Code: 4127X